The
Freekeh Cookbook

Healthy, Delicious, Easy-to-Prepare Meals with
America's Hottest Grain

The
Freekeh Cookbook

written and photographed by

BONNIE MATTHEWS

Skyhorse Publishing

Special thanks to my family, Linda, Diane, Melanie, Lindsay, and Brian. And finally, to Dr. Oz, who gave me my first break on his show.

Skyhorse Publishing books may be purchased in bulk at special discounts for sales promotion, corporate gifts, fund-raising, or educational purposes. Special editions can also be created to specifications. For details, contact the Special Sales Department, Skyhorse Publishing, 307 West 36th Street, 11th Floor, New York, NY 10018 or info@skyhorsepublishing.com.

Skyhorse® and Skyhorse Publishing® are registered trademarks of Skyhorse Publishing, Inc.®, a Delaware corporation.

Visit our website at www.skyhorsepublishing.com.

10 9 8 7 6 5 4 3 2 1

Library of Congress Cataloging-in-Publication Data is available on file.

ISBN: 978-1-62873-616-8
e-ISBN: 978-1-62873-970-1

Printed in China

introduction

A home cook's take on whole-grain recipes

I've been asked many times how I found this whole grain with a funny name. The answer is that it sort of found me—and just when I needed it most. Although my chance meeting with this ancient grain occurred as part of a whole-body transformation in my mid-forties, my history with food began much earlier.

Growing up with a food culture

I grew up in a Southern household where my father was a great home cook. To this day, I still have no idea how he made such perfectly golden, crispy fried chicken. Food was a festive part of our household, especially around the holidays. My dad was a self-taught baker and made amazing cakes, cookies, and fudge.

My father had a bit more patience than I, and I remember watching him so very meticulously create every single rose out of icing for my sister's wedding cake one summer. I, on the other hand, preferred simply to eat the cake, rather than make it! And that's where I got into trouble.

Over the years, I continued to pack on the pounds as I navigated through my young adult life. College pressures soon gave way to work deadlines as I put my fine arts degree to use at a design firm and, later, as a freelance illustrator. By the time I was 43 I weighed upward of 270 pounds.

A feeling something had to change

I was proud of the career I had built as a children's book illustrator, but I began to realize I needed to move more and sit less if I was going to keep a heart attack at bay. My dad and my creative inspiration had suffered four heart attacks before he was 50 years old. As I began creeping closer to that age, my doctor told me I was on my way to having one as well if I didn't start eating better.

It was then, around 2007, when I decided to break the family tradition; the "Matthews Way" had always just been to accept that we were all overweight. But suddenly, for the first time in my life, I made a conscious decision to actually pay attention to what I was eating. There have been days when I would have traded anything to have my dad back in the kitchen, preparing a batch of his neighborhood-famous chocolate fudge, but there have been many other days of learning to feed my new lifestyle.

How a food store helped me lose weight

Just as my weight-loss journey was taking off, the economy was making its 2008 downturn, and children's book illustration projects were hard to come by. Newly single with a mortgage to pay on my own, I took a part-time job as a food-demo cook at Trader Joe's. It was this job that literally saved my life.

Tucked in the back corner of that store, I worked to create recipes that showcased our products and taught customers how to do the same. What I got in return was a new appreciation for creating delicious recipes in a healthier way than I had in the past. And that's where I first discovered freekeh!

Any Trader Joe's customer who knows me will tell you I fell in love with this new product. I loved that it had high fiber and high protein, two things I was paying attention to on labels as part of my new lifestyle. And no cholesterol. Bingo! It was such a no brainer; you can use it as a substitute for rice in recipes. Rice has less than a third of the protein and fiber—even brown rice doesn't compare.

Fast-forward about two years, and lo and behold, I had burned off about 130 pounds through my newfound love for fitness and healthy cooking! I was literally melting away before my customers' eyes. The whole store and community were losing weight, too! Everyone was inspired and eating healthier. It was awesome! They said, "You should have your own cooking show."

I ended up being featured on *The Dr. Oz Show* in 2010 and celebrated my weight loss story. As part of my segment, I shared some of my healthy recipes, and many included freekeh. That is when the freekeh buzz started in the United States. Dr. Oz whispered in my ear and said, "Get used to this, Bonnie, because you are going to be doing a lot more TV." Who knows? But he made me a Wellness Warrior blogger on their website, and my dream came true. I was able to inspire others and share my passion for healthy cooking and fitness with the nation.

Sadly for viewers, however, prior to the show being aired, Trader Joe's had discontinued freekeh due to poor sales. No one knew what it was yet—it was just a little too soon.

But I was determined to figure out how to get it back on store shelves. I thought, if I can help people to not be afraid of unfamiliar, healthy food and still enjoy eating and still lose weight, that would be awesome. Through a lot of channels in the natural food world, I met Troy DeSmet, president of Nature's Organic Grist. He, too, shared a passion for freekeh, and with hard work and determination, we formed Freekeh Foods. Through a lot of trial and error, we were able to produce freekeh organically in the United States in 2011 and hit store shelves in 2012.

About the book
I have created this book of recipes to inspire folks and encourage them to cook freekeh, not just as a plain side dish, but as a marriage with vegetables and spices as one-pot meals like lemon dill chicken, or a great side dish like Mandarin freekeh salad. Because of my art background, I truly love color and texture and flavor—food is really like another art form that should be enjoyed and shared. I had decided when I was in the process of losing all that weight that I was not going to allow food to be an enemy—that I wanted it to still be pleasurable and not "drink my way to weight loss" using shakes or pills. This book shows off some healthy ways to enjoy food that you can share with friends, divide up to take to work and save you time, and even help get your kids to eat whole grains in foods that they will have fun trying!

In memory of my brother, Larry, my mom, and my dad
and for my friend Ann Marie—
all of whom remind me to make time to share great food and conversation
with the ones I love. Both are to be savored.

—Bonnie

Contents

I am not a trained chef, so I hope that these recipes are approachable for any level of cook. Many ingredients I share in the book can be found in most grocery stores or health food stores. I mention a lot of ingredients from Trader Joe's since I know their products so well, but many of them can certainly be found in other places as well. I don't cook with a lot of processed "white" sugar, or white flour. Instead, I cook "clean" and share some alternatives that may be healthier options. I truly believe that one of the reasons for the obesity epidemic in this nation is that foods contain so many additives and chemicals and are so overly processed that our bodies are not able to handle them or even comprehend that they are "food." In this book, there are many vegetables and spices that help to add lots of essential nutrients, vitamins, and minerals.

The story of behind freekeh

Freekeh is pronounced "free-kah" by most standards. But it's also called "frikeh" or "farik" in Arabic. While freekeh is relatively new in the United States, it has been a culinary staple of the Middle East for centuries. Nearly every time I go to New York, I get into a cab and ask the driver, "Have you ever had freekeh?" and nearly every single person says, "Of course, of course . . . ." Many drivers I've had were from Palestine, Egypt, and Lebanon. They all grew up on it and were so proud to share the stories of their mothers and their grandmothers talking about how they prepared it this way and that.

Freekeh is truly a Levantine cuisine—dating back to Syria, Jordan, Lebanon, Palestine, and Egypt. It's considered an ancient grain, so ancient, in fact, that it was mentioned in the Bible, though not by name. Leviticus 2:14 reads, "If you bring a grain offering of firstfruits to the Lord, offer crushed heads of new grain roasted in the fire." This was likely a very similar grain— perhaps roasted barley—whereas most freekeh today is produced using durum wheat.

So what is freekeh, you ask? Well, it's a roasted cereal grain that, as mentioned, dates back to Biblical times. Legend has it that two villages had a conflict and had burned each other's crops of grain in spring while they were still young and green. Once the conflict was over, they were left with no crops, only heads of roasted grain. They decided to rub the burned parts off and cook up what was left, and that is how freekeh became a "first offering" of the spring harvest. It cooks in water similarly to rice, in about 25 minutes. Because of this process, freekeh has a wonderful chewy texture and a slightly smoky, rich taste that is unlike any other grain.

Freekeh refers to the process of roasting baby wheat. The word "freekeh" or "farik" means "to rub" in Arabic—which refers to the farmers who used to harvest the durum wheat while the grain was still green and grass-like. They would cut it and pile it on the ground and light it on fire. The stalks and chaff would burn off, but the seeds didn't burn due to the high moisture content. They would then thrash or rub the grain and then cool it. Once they did that, freekeh was ready to be prepared into meals. Freekeh has been found in recipes dating back to the thirteenth century and is consumed in similar dishes even today using exotic spices, such as cumin, coriander, and cinnamon. It's often paired with meats, such as lamb and chicken.

An Egyptian cab driver in New York City told me his grandmother would make freekeh with cumin, onions, and coriander and top it with roasted chicken. Freekeh is often prepared with fewer meat-based and more vegetable-based mezze dishes, or with roasted meat served on top of the freekeh, like my cab driver discussed.

Nutrition behind the freekeh

Freekeh's been touted as a superfood by Chef Jamie Oliver and is gaining kudos because of its unique nutritional profile and interesting texture. Vandana R. Sheth, RDN, DCE, spokesperson for the Academy of Nutrition and Dietetics, said, "It's higher in protein, fiber, vitamins, minerals, and lower in glycemic index" as compared to other grains.

Because freekeh has more protein and fiber as compared to white rice or even brown rice, it's a great option to substitute in recipes that call for rice. It's been compared in the media to quinoa, since freekeh contains the same amount of protein per serving, which is 6 grams. And though freekeh does contain some gluten, the levels are very low—100 parts per million. To be completely gluten-free freekeh would need to fall below 20 ppm.

Toby Amidor, registered dietician and author, writes, "Freekeh is a whole grain and can help folks meet the USDA Dietary Guidelines, which recommends to make half your daily grain whole. One half-cup cooked provides around 130 calories, 6 grams of protein, and 1 gram of fat. It's a rich source of the mineral manganese, providing close to three-quarters of the daily recommended dose. It also offers a hefty dose of fiber, magnesium, and phosphorus."

Other notables are getting on the freekeh train, including America's favorite doctor, Dr. Oz. He's talked about it several times since I introduced it to him and listed it as a good lean protein option on his website. Kim Lyons, celebrity fitness trainer formerly of the hit show, *The Biggest Loser*, has freekeh listed on her "10 Day Fat Flush Diet" because it's such a good healthy carb. Lots of fitness folks are jumping on board, like Shawn T and the folks at Livestrong.com, because of the good protein and fiber it delivers as compared to brown rice and other grains. It's gaining more popularity in the media, and because of that, it's showing up on store shelves more and more nationwide.

Dieticians at Mercy Medical Center in Baltimore are even promoting freekeh as a rice replacement for their patients who have diabetes, since freekeh is low-glycemic. ShopRite dieticians are excited to be sharing information with their customers about its health benefits, along with many others nationwide.

Food trends

So freekeh's good for you, ok. But what about the flavor; does it taste good? You betcha! Chefs are adding it to their menus in trendy restaurants across America. You can find it in Brooklyn's trendy little Franny's restaurant, and, in New Jersey, they have a freekeh pizza at Dino's Cucina. Owner Chet Simunovich saw it on *The Dr. Oz Show* and decided to start experimenting with it, and his customers really like it.

There are so many healthy food trends in the United States, it's no wonder freekeh is being touted as "The Next Quinoa" by *Functional Ingredients Magazine*. And although quinoa is a superfood as well, it's had a backlash due to the unpopular effects on its native Bolivia because of over-exportation. Also, the global demand for quinoa has become an issue for many chefs who have had it on their menus and can no longer obtain it. The good news is, a lot of freekeh is being produced in the United States as well as Jordan and Australia, so supplying it is not an issue if it ends up exploding as quinoa has in the past few years.

Freekeh is the trendy "new" ancient grain. It's becoming easier to find on the store shelves nationwide. Several brands of freekeh on store shelves are U.S.-grown organic and non-GMO varieties. Look for it near the rice and other grains. All freekeh is 100 percent whole grain and comes in a whole berry, a cracked variety that takes less time to cook, and a flour. Freekeh grains can be found in many Whole Foods stores, Sprouts, ShopRite, Mother's Markets, health food stores, and ethnic grocery stores, as well as online. There are many private-label blends coming out now, too, including one by Rice Select®, which has freekeh in a blend of ancient grains. You'll also find freekeh in a vegetarian burger at Trader Joe's in their freezer case. The freekeh flour currently is only being sold online at www.freekeh-foods.com.

Stop reading this and get cooking!

I hope you will enjoy this book as much as I did creating it, tasting it, and photographing it for you. It's been quite a journey, and I'm excited to share this with you. I hope you are inspired to cook in some new ways with some ingredients you may not have tried in the past, like gaujilla peppers or coconut oil. I hope I have provided some recipes that will get you thinking about cooking with freekeh and other grains in general as an integral part of a meal, rather than just a blob of white as a boring side dish. I hope this book ignites your senses and interests you in exploring new ways to think about healthy cooking and enjoying it with your friends and family. I hope you invite freekeh to your table soon, and you can talk about it and make your own stories about freekeh. After all, food and conversation go hand in hand. Enjoy!

Cheers to your health,
Bonnie

chapter 1

mornings and in-betweens

meals to start your day right—
and snacks for that afternoon
energy boost

huevos rancheros

A nice recipe for weekends! There's an endless variety of toppings you can add to this traditional Mexican midmorning fare. Of course, it's usually prepared using Mexican-style rice and fried corn tortillas. Try serving it with a red and green chili sauce or tomatillo sauce, or top with queso fresco—sometimes called Mexican farmer's cheese.

makes: 6-8 servings (or take half of the filling and use in the breakfast burritos recipe on page 30)

1 cup cracked freekeh
6 eggs, or 1 per serving
1 15.5-ounce can of pinto or black beans, rinsed and drained
1 package of soft tortillas—multigrain, flour, or corn
½ sweet red pepper, diced
½ yellow pepper, diced

½ onion, diced
2 garlic cloves, minced (or about 1 teaspoon jarred, minced)
1 cup salsa, plus more for topping if desired
½ teaspoon jalapeno diced and seeded, or ½ guajillo pepper diced and seeded (for extra flavor and heat)
olive oil or other cooking oil

In a saucepan, empty 1 cup freekeh into 2½ cups water and bring to a boil. Reduce heat; add in the garlic and ¼ cup of the salsa, then cover. Simmer on medium heat for 20–25 minutes, until the water has been absorbed and the freekeh is tender.

While the freekeh is cooking, add olive oil to a skillet and heat up over medium heat. Add in diced peppers, diced onion, and hot peppers if you are using them. Cook until onions are translucent. Add in the remaining salsa, beans, and the cooked freekeh. Stir ingredients until mixed and remove from heat, cover, and set aside. Add salt and pepper to taste.

In a separate saucepan, heat up oil on medium-high heat. Fry eggs over easy and set aside until you have enough made to serve one per person.

Place bean and freekeh mixture on the plate and top with the fried egg. Add additional toppings, such as diced avocado, salsa fresca, or hot sauce, and eat immediately.

zucchini raisin muffins

preheat oven: 350°
makes: 12 regular-size muffins or 8 large muffins

2½ cups freekeh flour
1⅓ cups coconut palm sugar or other
    granulated sugar
2 teaspoons baking soda
½ teaspoon nutmeg
2½ teaspoons cinnamon
2 teaspoons allspice
pinch of salt

2 teaspoons vanilla extract
⅓ cup vegetable oil
3 cups grated fresh zucchini
⅔ cup melted butter or Earth Balance® buttery
    spread
1 cup raisins, dried cranberries, or dried
    currants

optional: add 1 cup chopped pecans or walnuts to the dough

In a large bowl, mix together sugar, salt, eggs, vanilla, and vegetable oil. Stir in grated zucchini and the melted butter.

Add in the flour and baking soda a little at a time, stirring in between pouring. Once all the flour and baking soda is mixed in, add the cinnamon, nutmeg, and allspice. Fold in dried fruit, and nuts if desired.

In a lined muffin tin (or use silicone muffin containers as shown in photo), fill nearly to the top with batter. Bake for about 25–30 minutes or until a toothpick has been inserted and comes out fairly clean.

Cool muffins before storing.

optional: see page 192 for a yummy goat cheese frosting if you want to add this next time you bake them!

freekeh with coconut milk and vanilla yogurt

I absolutely love oatmeal, but sometimes I like to switch it up and have a warm bowl of freekeh for breakfast. The chewy texture is a welcome change. I use half water and half light coconut milk and a touch of vanilla extract to give it a rich flavor. Add a little maple syrup or sweeten with zero-calorie stevia. Top with your favorite vanilla yogurt and fresh berries! It gives you lots of energy and sticks with you all the way until lunchtime. Truth be told, I eat this after a workout sometimes, too, or for an afternoon snack!

rosemary sage crackers
with sunflower seeds

preheat oven: 375°
makes: 12–14 rectangular crackers

2 cups freekeh flour
1 teaspoon ground rosemary
1 teaspoon ground sage or rubbed sage
1 cup water (or more as needed)
dash of cayenne pepper
½ teaspoon sea salt
¾ cup extra virgin olive oil
½ cup sesame seeds (optional)
½ cup sunflower seeds

optional toppings: grated parmesan cheese and/or chia seeds

In a bowl, mix flour, rosemary, sage, cayenne pepper, sea salt, and sesame seeds (optional) with a spoon.

Slowly stir in oil and mix until it becomes evenly crumbly. Add in water until mixture is moistened and will stick together in your hand when you clump it together.

Line a baking tray with parchment paper. Place dough in the middle of the pan and tamp down with the palm of your hand. Continue adding more dough until the entire pan is filled with dough that is about ⅛ inch thick or less. Be careful not to make it too thin; otherwise, the dough will begin to crack. If this occurs, simply tamp down with fingertips to remove cracks.

Once flattened out on the paper, with a sharp knife, carefully score the crackers in 2-inch strips the length of the pan. Then do the same thing in the opposite direction to the desired length of the crackers. You can make them square, or about 4-inch strips for dipping. Leave the outer edges along the pan rustic. Sprinkle with sunflower seeds.

Bake for about 15–20 minutes or until the edges are golden brown. Turn oven off and let sit in the oven for another 5 minutes to dry out. Remove and let cool. Crackers will harden more as they cool. Keep for a day only, wrapped lightly in tin foil.

freekeh fuel energy balls

The ingredients are filled with nutrients that will boost your energy. A great little portable snack for your gym bag or to take on a hike.

makes: 40 small energy balls

1 8-ounce package cracked freekeh (1 cup dry, or about 2 cups cooked)
2 tablespoons coconut oil
1½ cups creamy peanut butter (I really love Once Again All Natural Peanut Butter® because the oils don't separate from the peanut butter like most natural peanut butters)
3 cups oats (uncooked)
½ cup mini chocolate chips or cocoa nibs
2 cups raw pepita seeds, unsalted (green pumpkin seeds)

½ cup dried cranberries or tart dried cherries
½ cup ground flaxseed meal or substitute ¾ cup chia seeds
½ cup almond meal
½ to1 cup brown rice syrup (start with ½ cup and add in more as needed to moisten)
½ cup raw sunflower seeds (or toasted)
1 cup raw coconut flakes, no sugar added
1 cup raw sesame seeds (look for these in bulk bins—they are less expensive there)

hint: 2 large mixing bowls will help you with this recipe.

hint: disposable latex or vinyl gloves are helpful for making these—look for these at the pharmacy, or at the hardware store in the paint aisle.

In a saucepan, empty 1 cup freekeh into 2½ cups water and bring to a boil. Reduce heat, cover, and simmer for 20–25 minutes until the water has been absorbed and the freekeh is tender. Once cooked, remove from heat and cool in the refrigerator about 20–30 minutes.

Empty freekeh into a large mixing bowl. Add all dry ingredients and mix with hands. Blend thoroughly so that the ingredients are evenly dispersed. Split the mixture into two bowls.

Pour the ingredients into bowls evenly and mix by hand until they are blended well. If your peanut butter is too hard, you may want to warm it in the microwave or in a saucepan first to soften before adding. Once mixed, try forming the ingredients into a small 1-inch ball. Add in a little more brown rice syrup if it's too dry. Taste-test mixture and add other ingredients to your liking.

Roll into 1-inch balls or form into bars. Place in airtight containers for up to two weeks in the refrigerator.

hint: if you are making them into bars, place waxed paper in between layers, and you can freeze them for up to a month in an airtight container.

warm breakfast freekeh with berries

A nice spring breakfast is awesome on the back porch with a hearty bowl of freekeh. Try cooking it in rice milk or almond milk instead of water. Top with fresh raspberries, vanilla yogurt, and walnuts for a little added protein. Great fuel to start the day.

pumpkin muffins with chocolate chips

preheat oven: 375°
makes: 12 regular-size muffins or 8 large muffins

1½ cups freekeh flour
1 cup oats, uncooked
1 cup coconut palm sugar or other
   granulated sugar
2 teaspoons baking powder
½ teaspoon baking soda
1½ teaspoons cinnamon
1 teaspoon vanilla
½ teaspoon ground ginger

1 teaspoon allspice
1 15-ounce can of pumpkin
3 tablespoons olive oil or canola oil
2 large eggs, slightly beaten
1½ cups almond milk or regular milk
½ cup semi-sweet or dark chocolate
   chips or cocoa nibs
dash of sea salt

In a large bowl, add all dry ingredients and blend with a large spoon. Add in pumpkin, oil, milk, vanilla, and eggs. Mix dry and wet ingredients with a spoon. Stir in chocolate chips.

Place paper liners in muffin tins or use silicone muffin holders as shown. Fill muffin tins evenly and bake for about 18–25 minutes or until done. Check to see if muffins are done by inserting a toothpick. If it comes out clean, the muffins are done.

breakfast burrito

makes: 6-8 burritos (or use half of the filling and save the rest for huevos rancheros for breakfast another day; see page 16)

1 cup cracked freekeh
4 eggs, scrambled
1 15.5-ounce can of pinto or black beans, rinsed and drained
1 package of soft tortillas—multigrain, flour, or corn
½ sweet red pepper, diced
½ yellow pepper, diced

½ onion, diced
2 garlic cloves, minced (or about 1 teaspoon jarred, minced)
1 cup salsa plus more for topping if desired
½ jalapeno or guajillo pepper (for extra flavor and heat), seeded and diced
olive oil or other cooking oil

options: top with diced avocado, salsa fresca, or wedges of lime

In a saucepan, empty 1 cup freekeh into 2½ cups water and bring to a boil. Reduce heat, add the garlic and ¼ cup of the salsa, and cover. Simmer on medium heat for 20–25 minutes, until the water has been absorbed and the freekeh is tender.

While the freekeh is cooking, add olive oil to a skillet and heat up over medium heat. Add diced peppers, diced onion, and hot peppers if you are using them. Cook until onions are translucent. Add in the remaining salsa, beans, and the cooked freekeh. Stir ingredients until mixed, and remove from heat, cover, and set aside. Add salt and pepper to taste.

In a separate saucepan over medium heat, add oil. Pour in beaten eggs and scramble until cooked to desired texture. Add salt and pepper to taste. Cover and set aside.

While the eggs are cooking, heat up tortillas in a separate skillet on medium heat.

Place tortilla on plate and add the freekeh and bean mixture to the center of tortilla. Add scrambled eggs and top with additional salsa or salsa fresca. Top with diced avocado.

breakfast freekeh with peanut butter and banana cooked in almond milk

I make this two ways depending on my mood. Sometimes I cook the freekeh in almond milk, and then just add a dollop of creamy peanut butter in the bowl. Other times, I actually stir the peanut butter in the saucepan right when the freekeh is done cooking. It's much creamier that way. Banana works great on top. This makes a nice lunch to take to work.

banana pancakes

Cooking these in coconut oil gives the pancakes a great flavor and a nice crispy edge!

makes: about 12 medium pancakes

2–3 ripe bananas, peeled and smashed
½ cup almond milk, unsweetened (you may
    need to add a little more if the batter is too
    thick to pour)
½ teaspoon vanilla extract
2 eggs, beaten
1 cup freekeh flour
1½ teaspoons baking powder

¼ teaspoon salt
2 tablespoons olive oil, vegetable oil, or melted
    butter
coconut oil for cooking (works great for crispy
    edges since it can be heated higher than
    vegetable oil)
optional toppings: maple syrup, agave nectar,
    or honey

In a small bowl, mash the bananas and set aside.

In a larger bowl, add the beaten eggs, almond milk, and vanilla extract, and mix together with a spoon. Stir in the bananas, olive oil, and a little of the flour at a time. Continue adding until all the flour is stirred in well. Add the baking powder and mix well.

In a skillet, on medium-high heat, add enough coconut oil to coat the bottom of the skillet.

Using a measuring cup, pour in about ¼ cup of batter into the skillet. Make about three pancakes at a time, shaking the skillet after you pour each time, to make sure the coconut oil gets underneath so they don't stick. Cook until the sides of the pancakes begin to brown, and then carefully turn them over and cook another minute or two until done.

Remove from pan and set aside on a paper towel-lined plate.

You may need to add a little more oil each time before placing more batter in the skillet. Repeat and continue to cook more pancakes.

Serve with maple syrup, agave nectar, or honey. Add more bananas on top if desired.

hint: super good with a little all-natural peanut butter smeared on top, too!

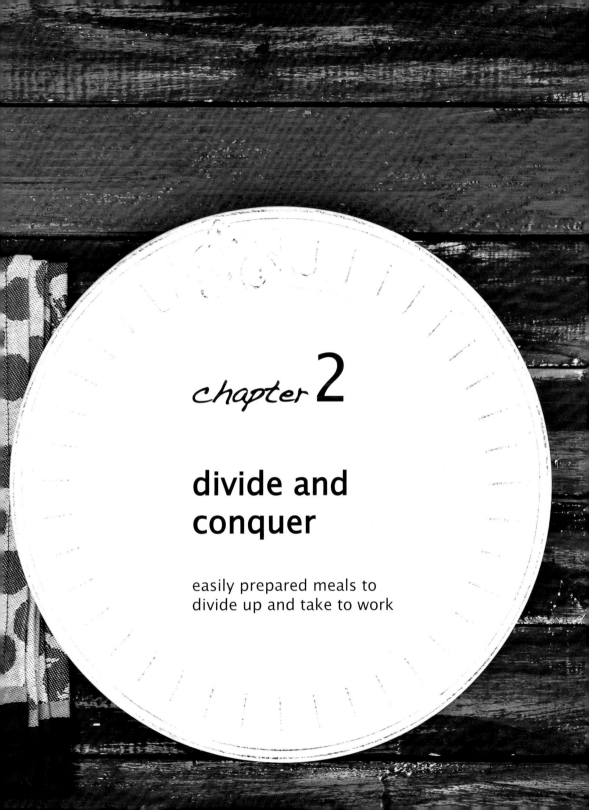

chapter 2

divide and conquer

easily prepared meals to
divide up and take to work

shrimp with Brussels sprouts, carrots, and freekeh

makes: 4-6 servings

1½ cups shrimp (about 12–16 medium-sized
    frozen shrimp, thawed and deveined)
2 cups Brussels sprouts, sliced in half
½ cup freekeh, uncooked
1 cup water or vegetable broth
2 cups carrots, diced
2 lemons, juiced
¼ teaspoon cumin
¼ teaspoon garlic powder
¼ teaspoon red chili flakes, or less if desired

pinch of cinnamon
¼ teaspoon thyme
¼ teaspoon oregano
pinch of turmeric
½ teaspoon dried ginger or ¼ teaspoon fresh
    ground ginger
drizzle of extra virgin olive oil
fresh squeezed lemon, to taste
1 tablespoon butter
fresh cracked pepper, sea salt

Pour water and freekeh in a saucepan and bring to a boil, cooking for 1 minute. Reduce heat to low. Add ½ teaspoon of garlic. Cover and simmer for about 25 minutes until the freekeh is tender. Once cooked, remove from heat and set aside.

While the freekeh is cooking, remove the small hard stem from the ends of the Brussels sprouts and slice them in half. Place them in a saucepan with about ½ inch of water. Cover and bring to a boil. Then reduce heat and steam until fork-tender but not mushy. Peel carrots if desired, then dice them into bite-sized pieces. Add them to a saucepan with ½ inch of water. Cover and bring to a boil. Then reduce heat and steam until fork-tender. You can also do both of these steps in the microwave in a bowl with a little water if you prefer.

Add vegetables to a large skillet drizzled with olive oil and heat on medium. Add all the spices except for the turmeric and stir to coat vegetables evenly. Add the fully cooked freekeh and cook further for about 1 minute. Then reduce heat to low.

Devein the shrimp and pat dry. Heat olive oil on high heat, in a small skillet. Toss in shrimp to cook. After about a minute, add in a tablespoon of butter and a pinch of turmeric powder and dried ginger. Add a little salt and garlic powder and turn off heat. Shrimp will cook rapidly, in about 2 minutes, and will be done when pink and firm. Once done, remove shrimp from heat and add them to the freekeh and vegetable mixture immediately. Add fresh squeezed lemon and gently stir in. Add fresh cracked pepper and salt to taste. Serve immediately.

optional: try adding fresh-wilted kale, too.

Italian chicken with sun-dried tomatoes and wilted spinach

I shared this recipe at my "Get Bon Wellness Retreat" two years ago. If I have sweet red or yellow peppers on hand, those are great in this recipe, too. Simply add them in when you add the onions.

makes: 4 servings

1 8-ounce package cracked freekeh (1 cup dry, or about 2 cups cooked)
2½ cups chicken broth or water
2 chicken breasts, skinless and boneless, cut into chunks
2 tablespoons extra virgin olive oil
1–2 tablespoons Earth Balance® or butter
8 garlic cloves, chopped
1 medium yellow onion, chopped in large chunks

1 cup sun-dried tomatoes, julienne cut
10 cremini mushrooms, sliced (or use sliced portobello mushrooms)
1 6-ounce package fresh spinach, prewashed
¾ cup crumbled goat cheese
2 tablespoons Parmesan or asiago cheese, grated
¼ cup pine nuts or chopped walnuts
oregano, red chili flakes, black pepper to taste

Pour chicken broth or water and the freekeh in a saucepan and bring to a boil, cooking for 1 minute. Reduce heat to low. Cover and simmer for about 25 minutes until the freekeh is tender. Once cooked, remove from heat.

Add olive oil to a large skillet and heat up on medium. Add chunks of chicken, oregano, red chili flakes, and black pepper. After about 6 minutes, add Earth Balance® or butter and continue cooking until chicken is golden brown. Remove chicken from skillet and set aside.

In the same skillet, drizzle more olive oil and add garlic, onion, sun-dried tomatoes, and mushrooms. Cook for 5–7 minutes over medium heat until tender. Toss the chicken back into the skillet, add the entire bag of spinach, and stir. Continue to stir until the spinach is still bright green but wilted. Remove the skillet from the heat. Add goat cheese and Parmesan cheese, stirring until chicken is coated. Add in the cooked freekeh and stir. In a separate small skillet, heat olive oil and add in the pine nuts. Stir constantly until the pine nuts are lightly browned and remove from heat immediately. Sprinkle pine nuts into the main dish and serve immediately.

avocado salad with fire-roasted corn and tomato

I adapted this recipe from a friend at the gym. She used farro with it originally, but she recalls the original version called for millet or barley. The freekeh works well with it because it absorbs all that lime juice! Feel free to add some grilled shrimp that's been marinated in lime zest, orange juice, and garlic, too!

makes: 6–8 servings (a great amount for lunch for a week!)

1 8-ounce package cracked freekeh (1 cup dry, or about 2 cups cooked)
½ cup water or vegetable broth
4 good shakes of salt (I cranked my salt grinder 4 times)
1 large jalapeno, seeded and diced
1½ to 2 cups fire-roasted corn (I bought the Trader Joe's Frozen Fire-Roasted Corn®, and thawed it; use fresh or canned sweet corn as a substitute)
⅓ cup cilantro, diced, stems included
2 tablespoons green onions, diced
5 limes, juiced
2 cups grape or Little Spendito tomatoes, quartered
2 avocados, diced (or more if you have them!)

Pour water or vegetable broth and the freekeh in a saucepan and bring to a boil, cooking for 1 minute. Reduce heat to low. Cover and simmer for about 25 minutes until the freekeh is tender. Once cooked, remove from heat and let cool.

Thaw corn, or if using canned corn, drain the liquid and place in a large bowl. Add diced green onion, tomatoes, and the diced pepper. Add the cooled freekeh and mix gently. Add the lime juice, salt, pepper, and cilantro. Serve at room temperature or chilled.

note: the amount of lime juice you can squeeze out really varies depending on the lime. If they are small and firm, it may be harder to extract enough juice. Look for larger, softer limes that you can squeeze with ease! In a pinch, use store-bought Key lime juice.

stir-fry with shrimp and Hoisin sauce

I think it's safe to say that most of us have made a few stir-fries in our lifetime. There are so many great veggies out there and quite a few decent store-bought, premade stir-fry sauces in the markets, it would be easy to make this every week for a year and still come up with new versions of it! Use this as a launch pad to get creative. Try adding new veggies you are not familiar with, like sugar snap peas, bok choy, Chinese eggplant, and purple cabbage. Keep a bag of frozen precooked shrimp in your freezer for those nights you are working late and want to make something fast with all the leftover veggies in your fridge.

makes: 6 servings easily!

1 8-ounce package cracked freekeh (1 cup dry, or about 2 cups cooked)
2½ cups water or vegetable broth
8–10 frozen precooked shrimp, thawed and patted dry
a handful of broccoli crowns, with most of stem removed
a large handful of fresh sugar snap peas or snow peas
shredded cabbage (purple or white or both)
shredded carrot
½ onion, diced large (or use diced green onions)
handful of sliced sweet peppers, any color
about ½ cup or more of Hoisin sauce
3–5 cloves of garlic, diced
toasted sesame seed oil, coconut oil, or vegetable oil
chopped peanuts
fresh cilantro to garnish

Pour water or vegetable broth and the freekeh in a saucepan and bring to a boil, cooking for 1 minute. Reduce heat to low. Cover and simmer for about 25 minutes until the freekeh is tender. Once cooked, remove from heat and let cool.

Drizzle sesame seed oil to coat the bottom of a large wok or skillet. Heat skillet on high, being careful not to let the oil burn. Toss in the vegetables and garlic. Cook for about 3–5 minutes, stirring constantly. Reduce temperature to medium. Once the vegetables begin to get tender but are still crisp, toss in the shrimp and drizzle in the Hoisin sauce. Continue to cook for another minute or two. Mix in the cooked freekeh in the same skillet, or simply place freekeh on a plate and top with the stir-fry. Garnish with chopped peanuts and chopped cilantro.

timesaver: the volume in the ingredients list can vary depending on what you have in your refrigerator. Many of these vegetables can be found prechopped at the salad bars of Whole Foods or other stores.

kale walnut cranberry salad

I just love tangy anything. Especially when it's offset by crunchy and sweet! That's why I love this basic, good salad with the nuts, vinegar, and dried fruits. Try this recipe with Montmorency cherries instead of cranberries, too! They are high in antioxidants and have anti-inflammatory properties, which are good for muscle soreness and helping fight heart disease, according to Dr. Oz. You can find them at Trader Joe's and many health food stores in bulk bins.

makes: 4–6 servings

1 8-ounce package cracked freekeh
   (1 cup dry, or about 2 cups cooked)
2½ cups water or vegetable broth
½ cup dried cranberries or dried tart cherries
3 cups chopped curly kale
½ cup crumbled goat cheese (or log goat
   cheese, crumbled)
1 cup raw walnuts
1 cup shredded carrots (get some off the salad
   bar if you only want a few!)

salt and pepper to taste

the dressing:
½ cup apple cider vinegar (or white balsamic
   vinegar)
3 tablespoons extra virgin olive oil
1 tablespoon honey mustard or Dijon mustard
2 tablespoons maple syrup

Whisk together dressing ingredients until blended.

Pour water and the freekeh in a saucepan and bring to a boil, cooking for 1 minute. Reduce heat to low. Cover and simmer for about 25 minutes until the freekeh is tender. Once cooked, remove from heat and set aside to cool.

Chop the kale and shred the carrots. Combine kale, carrots, cranberries, walnuts, and freekeh in a large bowl and mix with a spoon. Add in the dressing a little at a time to coat all ingredients. You may have some left over. Add the crumbled goat cheese last, and gently stir in—but not too much, or it will become too creamy.

Serve immediately or slightly chilled.

optional: want to make this a whole meal? Top with cold grilled chicken or some leftover rotisserie chicken. Dinner in 5 minutes never tasted so healthy!

curried chicken salad wraps

makes: about 8 wraps

2 tablespoons olive oil

1 8-ounce package cracked freekeh (1 cup
   dry, or about 2 cups cooked)

2½ cups chicken broth or water

¾ cup sliced almonds

1 granny smith apple with peel on,
   seeded and diced

½ cup Veganaise® or mayonnaise

½ cup Greek-style nonfat plain yogurt

½ teaspoon coriander

1 cup raisins

½ teaspoon turmeric spice

6–8 100 percent whole-grain tortilla or brown
   rice wraps

salt and cracked pepper to taste

marinade

1 pound chicken tenders or skinless, boneless
   chicken breasts

3 tablespoons curry powder

fresh cracked black pepper

¼ teaspoon ground cardamom

1 teaspoon cumin

2 dashes cayenne pepper

3 teaspoons garlic, diced

1 cup light coconut milk or nonfat plain yogurt

1 teaspoon mustard powder

1 teaspoon ground ginger

1 teaspoon turmeric

1 teaspoon coriander

salt and pepper to taste

In a large bowl, combine all marinade ingredients except for the chicken. Cut chicken into chunks, then add into the bowl and coat chunks thoroughly. Cover and place in refrigerator for at least an hour or overnight for a richer flavor. After marinating, heat in a large skillet over medium heat. Cook chicken in batches. Allow to cool thoroughly, refrigerating if necessary.

Pour chicken broth or water and freekeh in a saucepan and bring to a boil for 1 minute. Reduce heat to low. Cover and simmer for about 25 minutes until the freekeh is tender. Once the freekeh is cooked, place in a separate dish to cool in the refrigerator.

In a large bowl, add in the Veganaise®, apples, raisins, nuts, and remaining spices and mix. Add in the freekeh and chicken and toss together. Allow to chill. Serve chicken salad on top of a bed of greens that are dressed in apple cider vinegar and olive oil, or serve in your favorite tortilla as a wrap.

time saver: I have made this recipe using fresh Trader Joe's Curried Chicken Tenders®, which are absolutely succulent and delicious! Their chicken and meats are grown without any hormones, antibiotics, or additives. If you can swing it, free-range chicken is an even better choice—and not just for flavor! It's nice to know that the chickens are out in the sun having a happy outside life pecking at the earth and eating bugs.

roasted yams with chicken apple sausage and kale

When I was in second grade, my class did a unit on African recipes. I remember being in charge of cutting up yams—and my teacher complimenting me on my cooking prowess at such a young age. I used to be painfully shy when I was little. I truly think her taking notice of my joy of cooking gave me the confidence to keep pursuing my passion with food.

To make this a vegan recipe, simply use vegetable broth instead of chicken. Use Field Roast Rosemary Sage Sausage® or Tofurkey Sausage® instead. Look for them in the refrigerated section near the vegetarian foods. They are both vegan.

preheat oven: 375°
makes: 4-6 servings

1 8-ounce package cracked freekeh (1 cup dry, or about 2 cups cooked)
2½ cups chicken broth
1-2 red yams or sweet potatoes, scrubbed and cubed with skins on
1 package (6 links) chicken apple sausage, sliced in discs

½ bunch of fresh lacinato kale, also known as dinosaur kale (it has dark, flat leaves with a pebbly surface)
1 cup mushrooms, diced
fresh or dried sage and thyme to taste
olive oil, salt, and pepper to taste
1 cup dried cranberries or dried cherries
1 cup walnuts
optional: diced onion, sweet peppers

Pour 2½ cups of water and the freekeh in a saucepan and bring to a boil for 1 minute. Reduce heat to low. Cover and simmer for about 25 minutes until the freekeh is tender.

Place cubed yams or sweet potatoes in a bowl and add olive oil, tossing cubes to coat evenly. Place yams on a foil-lined baking sheet. Lightly cover with a piece of tin foil. Cook for about 25-30 minutes or until tender with a fork. Once done, remove from oven and set aside.

While the yams and freekeh are cooking, drizzle a little olive oil in a skillet on medium heat. Toss in sausage and brown. Remove sausage and set aside. In the same skillet, toss in mushrooms, spices, and kale. Sautée for a few minutes until the kale is slightly wilted—about 4 minutes. Once the freekeh and yams are cooked, add to the skillet. Mix in the cooked sausage, cranberries, and nuts.

tabbouleh wrap with red pepper hummus

There are so many great store-bought hummus varieties out there. Look for red pepper hummus for this recipe! It can be found in the refrigerator section near the specialty cheeses. Artichoke spread is also really yummy as an alternative. To make your own artichoke dip, start with a can of artichokes. Blend them in a food processor with extra virgin olive oil, plenty of fresh lemon juice, salt, parsley, good quality Parmesan cheese, a few cloves of garlic, and a dash of cayenne pepper. Done! This can keep in the refrigerator for up to five days.

makes: 6–8 servings

1 cup cracked freekeh (2 cups cooked)
2½ cups water or vegetable broth
2 cups flat-leaf parsley
½ cup fresh mint, chopped
handful of grape tomatoes, diced (I used Little Splenditos® from Trader Joe's—they are just so darn sweet!)
½ cup seedless cucumber, diced
3–4 tablespoons fresh lemon juice

3–4 garlic cloves, diced (or 3 teaspoons minced from jar)
salt and pepper to taste
extra virgin olive oil
store-bought red pepper hummus, or any kind of hummus you enjoy
whole-grain or multigrain wraps (I use whole grain with chia seeds in them!)

Pour water and the freekeh in a saucepan and bring to a boil, cooking for 1 minute. Reduce heat to low. Cover and simmer for about 25 minutes until the freekeh is tender. Once cooked, remove from heat and set aside to cool.

Add all ingredients in a large bowl and mix well with a spoon. Taste and adjust seasoning if needed.

For wraps, simply spread hummus on the wrap, add the tabbouleh mixture, and serve rolled-up or open-faced.

warm freekeh with carrots and za'atar seasoning

You may have had za'atar seasoning and not even known it! It's a blend of spices used in Middle Eastern recipes and often served on top of hummus or fresh pita bread. The most common blends contain a mixture of oregano, thyme, sesame seeds, salt, and sometimes sumac and marjoram.

It has a wonderful flavor that works great with vegetables and on top of hummus with olive oil and fresh lemon.

Food commentator Bonny Wolf of NPR just touted freekeh and za'atar on her list of food trend predictions for 2014 on the show "Weekend Edition." This recipe is a double-hitter for food trending, I guess!

Look for za'atar in the spice aisle, at any Middle Eastern grocery store, or online!

makes 4–6 servings

½ cup cracked freekeh, uncooked
1 cup vegetable broth or water
6–8 carrots, diced
2–3 cloves garlic, minced
about ½ cup feta cheese

3–4 tablespoons za'atar seasoning
    (more or less to taste)
extra virgin olive oil
dash of cayenne pepper

Pour water and the freekeh in a saucepan and bring to a boil, cooking for 1 minute. Reduce heat to low. Cover and simmer for about 7–8 minutes. Add in diced carrots and garlic and continue cooking until the carrots and freekeh are tender. Add liquid if necessary.

Remove from heat and mix in feta cheese, dash of cayenne pepper, and a little drizzle of olive oil. Add salt and pepper to taste and top with a little more za'atar seasoning. Serve with a squirt of fresh lemon if desired.

optional: add a can of chickpeas (also called garbanzo beans) to make a more complete meal with this dish. Simply drain and rinse the chickpeas and add them in once the freekeh and carrots are done. Cook for a few minutes until the chickpeas are warm, then follow remaining steps and serve.

broccoli salad with artichoke, tomato, and smoked sardines

Seriously a great go-to salad, no matter what time of day. This is one of my favorite meals after a hard workout. Laugh all you want about sardines, but they are packed with omega-3 fatty acids and are a delicious, inexpensive protein source.

makes: 4–6 servings

1 8-ounce package cracked freekeh (1 cup dry, or about 2 cups cooked)

2½ cups water or vegetable broth

1 large bunch of broccoli crowns, cut into bite-sized pieces

1 can of good-quality lightly smoked sardines packed in oil or water

1 12-ounce jar of marinated artichoke hearts (retain the liquid from the jar)

3–4 large tomatoes, cut into wedges (I splurged and used local heirloom)

good-quality grated Parmesan cheese

1 cup Kalamata olives or French herbed black olives (look for these on Mediterranean salad bars in the store)

a few tablespoons of white balsamic vinegar

Pour 2½ cups of water and the freekeh in a saucepan and bring to a boil for 1 minute. Reduce heat to low. Cover and simmer for about 25 minutes until the freekeh is tender. Once done, remove from heat and set aside to cool.

Take the broccoli crowns and place in a saucepan or steamer with about ½ inch of water. Cover and bring to a light boil. Then turn heat down to steam vegetables just until they turn bright. Once done, immediately remove from heat and drain the water out. Run cold water over them in the sink to stop the cooking process. Then drain and place them in a large bowl. Add all ingredients except the sardines. Add the liquid from the jar of artichokes and gently stir with a spoon. Add the sardines last, or arrange the fillets on top of the dish. Drizzle a little white balsamic vinegar if desired. Add fresh cracked pepper and a little extra Parmesan to serve.

Serve chilled.

Mandarin freekeh salad

Cabbage is fantastically crunchy and often overlooked. It adds great crunch to any salad.

makes: 4–6 servings

1 8-ounce package cracked freekeh (1 cup dry, or about 2 cups cooked)
2½ cups vegetable broth or water
2 cups fresh sugar snap peas, or snow peas, cut in half
½ head of a small purple cabbage, shredded
½ head of a small red cabbage, shredded
1 package shredded carrot
1–2 small cans Mandarin orange wedges, drained
1 cup sliced almonds (or substitute chopped peanuts or cashews)
1 bunch fresh cilantro, chopped (including the stems)
1–1½ cups Thai peanut sauce (I like San-J® brand because it has a nice kick)
4 teaspoons toasted sesame seed oil (or more if desired)
¼ cup seasoned rice vinegar

Pour 2½ cups of water and the freekeh in a saucepan and bring to a boil for 1 minute. Reduce heat to low. Cover and simmer for about 25 minutes until the freekeh is tender. Once cooked, remove from heat and place in a large bowl to cool.

Mix vegetables together in a large bowl with a spoon. Add the peanut sauce, toasted sesame seed oil, and rice vinegar. Mix gently. Add in the freekeh, cilantro, and nuts, stirring gently.

Serve room temperature or chilled.

optional: great with diced shrimp or tofu. Simply cook in a separate skillet with some sesame seed oil, allow to cool, and add it to the other ingredients. Frozen precooked shrimp also work great for this! Simply thaw out in cool water in the sink for a few minutes. Pat dry with a paper towel before cooking them.

for extra spice: add a few shakes of cayenne pepper, ginger, and garlic!

time saver: if you are in a rush, buy a bag of pre-shredded cabbage, or grab some off the salad bar.

tofu and baby spinach salad

This is a simple, healthy recipe that is satisfying but won't leave you feeling heavy. I like the Soy Vay® sauce on this, but use any kind of stir-fry or Thai peanut sauce you enjoy.

makes: 4 servings

1 8-ounce package cracked freekeh (1 cup
   dry, or about 2 cups cooked)
2½ cups vegetable broth or water
2–3 cloves of garlic, minced
1 12-ounce package extra-firm tofu
1 10-ounce bag baby spinach, prewashed
   (about 6 cups)
1 bunch of green onions

a handful of shredded carrots
sprinkle of sesame seeds (look for these on
   the salad bar)
¾ cup Soy Vay® sauce or any kind of stir-fry
   sauce
toasted sesame seed oil
fresh cracked pepper or white pepper

Pour water and the freekeh in a saucepan and bring to a boil, cooking for 1 minute. Reduce heat to low. Add minced garlic. Cover and simmer for about 15 minutes. Add a handful of shredded carrots, and continue to cook for another 10 minutes until the freekeh and carrots are tender. Once cooked, remove from heat and set aside to allow time to assemble the meal.

Slice the tofu into filets about ⅜-inch thick. Pat them dry with a paper towel. Drizzle toasted sesame seed oil in a skillet and heat up over medium heat. Place the tofu filets in the pan and cook on each side for about 2–4 minutes, then set aside on a paper towel-lined plate.

To serve, place a handful of fresh baby spinach in the center of a plate. Add about ½ cup of the freekeh and carrot mixture to the center. Place one or two pieces of tofu on the mixture. Top with diced green onion and drizzle with Soy Vay® sauce. Sprinkle sesame seeds on top and serve.

optional: for a crispier tofu, dredge the filet in rice flour first, then pan-fry in toasted sesame seed oil the same way until golden brown.

timesaver: get the shredded carrots off the salad bar.

optional: add a teaspoon of fresh minced ginger to freekeh while it's cooking.

tuna and freekeh salad with capers, lemon, and black olives on a bed of greens

Who needs the bread and mayo to enjoy tuna? Not me! I suggest canned light yellowfin or tonno tuna because I love the taste. It's much less dry than white albacore tuna. To save on a few calories, look for the tuna packed in spring water. Need to know what else to do with the remaining capers in the jar? Add them to your marinara sauce for the recipe on page 80.

makes: 4 servings

1 8-ounce package cracked freekeh (1 cup dry, or about 2 cups cooked)
2½ cups vegetable broth or water
6 cups romaine lettuce, chopped in bite-sized pieces (about 2 cups per serving)
1 5-ounce can of yellowfin or tonno tuna
1 cup Kalamata olives or French herbed black olives
4 tablespoons capers

½ cup slivered almonds
2–4 garlic cloves, minced fine
dusting of parmesan cheese
3 tablespoons lemon juice, fresh squeezed is best
⅓ cup extra virgin olive oil
fresh cracked pepper and sea salt or Himalayan pink salt

Pour 2½ cups of vegetable broth and the freekeh in a saucepan and bring to a boil for 1 minute. Reduce heat to low. Cover and simmer for about 25 minutes until the freekeh is tender. Once cooked, remove from heat and place into a large bowl to cool.

Whisk olive oil, garlic, and lemon juice together. Tastes even better if you let it sit a day in the fridge to flavor up!

Once freekeh is cooled, toss in tuna, capers, olives, almonds, and Parmesan, mixing gently with a spoon. Add in salt and fresh cracked pepper to taste. If you are using Kalamata olives, you will not need much additional salt. Drizzle dressing in a little at a time to taste. Serve on a bed of romaine lettuce.

optional: add grape or Little Splendido® tomatoes for extra color and flavor.

miso soup with enoki mushrooms and shrimp

Miso soup works great as a base for lots of ways to have a fast lunch to take to work—even faster if you use leftover freekeh that's already cooked. Or better yet, just make a batch and freeze it in portions for you to add to soups throughout the month.

In this recipe, I've added fresh enoki mushrooms. They have a very mild earthy flavor and are rich in cancer-fighting properties. Also included is nori seaweed, which has a high concentration of antioxidants, including vitamin C. Plus it contains a high amount of taurine, a substance known for aiding in controlling cholesterol. Nori also adds fiber and flavor.

makes: 4 servings at a time to keep for workweek lunches

4 packets of instant miso soup, prepared with water or vegetable broth
about 1½ cups cooked freekeh (or make ahead of time)
fresh enoki mushrooms (they are long and thin, usually packaged)

12 fully cooked shrimp
1 package tofu, diced in cubes
3–4 sheets nori seaweed, crumbled
garlic
fresh ginger, optional
5 green onions, diced, for garnish

In a large pot, heat up the prepared miso soup. Add in rinsed and thawed fully cooked shrimp and other ingredients except the green onion, and cook for another 2–3 minutes on low.

Let cool. Then portion out in containers so that there is an equal amount of freekeh, enoki mushrooms, and tofu.

To serve, simply reheat at work in the microwave until fully warm. Garnish with diced green onion.

timesaver: use leftover cooked freekeh and keep fully cooked frozen shrimp in the freezer to add to this soup in a jiffy!

other options: instead of seaweed, add fresh spinach, bok choy, or kale.

shredded chicken salad with pesto and sundried tomatoes

For an even faster meal, use leftover store-bought rotisserie chicken. And look for pesto in the refrigerated section of the store or in a jar near the Italian ingredients.

1 8-ounce package cracked freekeh (1 cup dry, or about 2 cups cooked)

2½ cups chicken broth or water

2 garlic cloves, minced fine

1 to 1½ cups fire-roasted, marinated sundried tomatoes in olive oil with herbs (I got mine off the Mediterranean salad bar at Whole Foods, or look for them in a jar in the grocery aisle)

½ cup fresh pesto

fresh baby spinach (or spring mix)

½ cup pine nuts, lightly toasted in olive oil until golden

cracked pepper

optional: extra Parmesan or Pecorino Romano cheese

Pour 2½ cups of vegetable broth and the freekeh in a saucepan and bring to a boil for 1 minute. Reduce heat to low. Add minced garlic. Cover and simmer for about 25 minutes until the freekeh is tender. Once cooked, remove from heat and place into a large bowl to cool.

In a small bowl, add the pesto and some of the herbed olive oil that came with the tomatoes. Mix well.

In a large bowl, add the cooled freekeh to the pesto and sundried tomato mixture. Mix gently with a spoon. Serve over fresh greens with pine nuts sprinkled on top. Add a dusting of fresh grated Parmesan or Pecorino Romano cheese and fresh cracked pepper.

If you want to make your own pesto, simply get a large bunch of basil and blend in ½ cup extra virgin olive oil, 4–6 garlic cloves, 1 cup pine nuts or walnuts, a dash of salt, and ½ cup Pecorino Romano or Parmesan cheese into a food processor until it becomes a thick paste.

chapter 3

kid-
friendly

traditional kid favorites
with a twist

turkey and freekeh meatballs

You can stretch out your dollar by adding in freekeh into the ground turkey for these meatballs. Use ground beef instead of turkey for another option.

preheat oven: 375°
makes: 14–16 meatballs

for the meatballs:

2 cups cooked freekeh

2–3 tablespoons olive oil

1 small onion, diced fine

1 egg, whisked

¼ cup of water or broth

1 pound ground turkey

2 tablespoons oatmeal flakes

4 teaspoons almond flour or whole-wheat flour

1 tablespoon oregano

¼ to ¾ cup Parmesan cheese

1 tablespoon onion powder

1 tablespoon garlic powder

3 tablespoons tomato paste

for the sauce:

1 24-ounce jar of marinara sauce

8 garlic cloves, diced fine

teaspoon of red pepper flakes

2 tablespoons capers

½ cup of water or broth

6 anchovy filets

10 fresh basil leaves, chopped

In a food processor, mix all sauce ingredients and set aside until meatballs are cooked.

In a large bowl, mix all meatball ingredients together, kneading mixture with your hands until everything is evenly blended. If it seems too dry, add a little more water or broth. Roll about 4 tablespoons of the mixture into a ball with your hands. Continue to make the balls and set on a plate. Wash hands thoroughly.

Pour about 4 tablespoons of olive oil in a nonstick skillet on medium heat. Add a few of the meatballs into the skillet using two spoons. Be careful not to break the meatballs! Add only a few at a time so you have enough room to turn them over. Brown them on all sides, turning them every 2 minutes or so. Once the meatballs are browned, remove them from the skillet and set aside. Repeat until they're all cooked.

Place the meatballs in a 9x12-inch nonstick casserole dish. Pour the sauce over the meatballs and cover with foil, creating a tight seal. Place in preheated oven and bake for about 45 minutes. After 45 minutes, remove the foil. By now, the meatballs should be plump from absorbing some of the sauce. If necessary, add a little more water, place foil back on, and cook another 10 minutes.

freekeh tacos

Freekeh is a nice substitute for rice in tacos or wraps. It adds more protein and integrates the grain into the recipe instead of as a side dish.

makes: 6 servings

1 8-ounce package cracked freekeh
   (1 cup dry, or about 2 cups cooked)
2½ cups vegetable broth
1 15-ounce can black beans
1 12-ounce jar of salsa (any kind you enjoy)
1 medium onion, diced
8 garlic cloves, diced
1 sweet yellow or red pepper, diced
about a teaspoon of jalapeno pepper, seeded
   and diced

2–4 tablespoons extra virgin olive oil
   (or other cooking oil)
1 teaspoon ground cumin
1½ tablespoons chipotle powder
   (or less, to taste)
1 teaspoon paprika
1 teaspoon onion powder
avocado, diced
tomato, diced
12 blue or white hard corn taco shells or soft
   corn tortillas

Pour 2½ cups of water and the freekeh in a saucepan and bring to a boil for 1 minute. Reduce heat to low. Stir in a few spoonfuls of the salsa, the onion and the chipotle powder. Cover and simmer for about 25 minutes until the freekeh is tender.

In a separate skillet, heat a drizzle of olive oil over medium heat. Toss in onion, jalapeno and sweet peppers, and garlic. Add cumin, onion powder, and paprika and cook for about 4–5 minutes until the onions are slightly translucent. Add in the beans and remaining salsa. Simmer for 4–6 minutes. Once the freekeh is done, add it to the other ingredients and cook for another minute or two. Fill taco shells or tortillas and serve with your favorite toppings.

optional: serve with shredded cabbage or lettuce, fire-roasted corn, and a fresh slice of lime to squeeze on just before eating! Another alternative is to add in vegetarian chorizo sausage to the recipe for even more added protein and spice. Add in to the skillet with the onions.

bbq freekeh franks-n-beans

This is not just for kids, let me tell you! I made it with some delicious local grass-fed beef mini-franks, and it was superb! You can dress this up any old way to suit your child's taste. To stretch it out, use two cans of beans and dice up the franks into bite-sized pieces.

makes: 6 more servings, depending on portion size

1 8-ounce package cracked freekeh
   (1 cup dry, or about 2 cups cooked)
2½ cups water or vegetable broth
1 14-ounce package cocktail-size mini beef
   franks (I used all-natural,
    grass-fed beef mini-links)

1 12-ounce can pink beans or pinto beans
   (I used Goya® pink beans) or use a
   12-ounce can of baked beans, drained and
   rinsed
½ to; ¾ cup mild barbeque sauce (I like good
   ole Open Pit by Kraft®)
3–4 tablespoons ketchup

Pour 2½ cups of broth or water and the freekeh in a large saucepan and bring to a boil for 1 minute. Reduce heat to low. Cover and simmer for about 25 minutes until the freekeh is tender.

If the beef franks are not fully cooked already, place them in a skillet with a little olive oil and brown them for about 3–5 minutes until done. If you are using fully cooked franks, simply place them directly in with the freekeh.

Add in all other ingredients and cook over medium heat until heated through—about 5 minutes.

stuffed zucchini boats

Using a little leftover cooked freekeh makes these a snap to put together for your little guys. Get the kids to help assemble them—they will love it! Have fun making a pirate's map placemat and have your kids draw in where the treasure is hidden. Tell them they can color it after they eat the zucchini boats!

makes: 6–8 medium-sized boats
preheat oven: 400°

1 cup fully cooked freekeh (use leftover)
3–4 medium zucchinis
1 cup water or vegetable broth

1 to 1½ cups marinara sauce (I used the Trader Joe's Roasted Garlic Marinara® for $1.99!)
¼ cup of Parmesan cheese, grated

Mix the cooked freekeh, marinara sauce, and a little of the Parmesan cheese together in a small bowl. Save some of the cheese for the topping.

Slice the zucchinis in half, and, with a spoon, scoop out a small portion of the center seeds to allow room for the filling.

Fill the zucchini halves with the freekeh mixture. Place the halves in a large roasting pan with about ¼ inch of water in it. Bake for about 20–25 minutes or until the zucchini is fork-tender. Sprinkle with the rest of the Parmesan cheese and cook for another few minutes until the cheese begins to melt.

optional: top with grated mozzerella cheese at the 20-minute mark and continue to cook until bubbling and brown.

enchilada stack

Need something fun to serve to the kids and their friends when they come over? Everyone can help make these.

makes: 4 stacks
preheat oven: 400°

½ cup cooked freekeh
2 tablespoons olive oil
about ¾ pound lean ground beef or ground
  turkey
1 packet taco seasoning (or fajita seasoning)
1 14.5-ounce can diced fire-roasted tomatoes
  in green chilis (or any kind of canned diced
  tomatoes)

½ medium onion, diced (about ½ cup)
½ green pepper, diced
12 corn tortillas or whole-wheat tortillas (use 3
  per stack)
1 12-ounce can refried beans
½ cup shredded cheddar cheese or queso
  fresco

In a large skillet, pour olive oil and add ground beef. Break up the beef into small chunks over medium heat so that it cooks evenly. Continue to cook through until there is no pink (about 5–7 minutes). Remove from heat and drain any excess fat.

In a separate skillet, add the onion, pepper, and a little olive oil. Cook onions on medium heat until they are tender and translucent. Add in the taco seasoning, meat, cooked freekeh, and canned tomatoes. Simmer on medium heat for about 2 minutes.

Spray two 9x12-inch casserole dishes. Begin making the stacks by placing 1 corn tortilla in the dish. With a large spoon, add the meat mixture. Then take another spoon and smear a second corn tortilla with refried beans and place on top of the meat stack, bean-side down. Add another layer of meat on top of that. Then smear another layer of beans on a third corn tortilla and place it face-down on the stack. Make 4 stacks of 3 tortillas each, 2 stacks per dish.

Cover lightly with foil and bake for about 20 minutes. Remove foil and add grated cheese. Continue to cook for a few minutes until the cheese has melted and the stacks are warm in the middle.

Serve with your favorite Mexican-style toppings, such as guacamole or diced avocado and salsa. Try using plain nonfat Greek yogurt instead of sour cream for a healthier option!

side options: corn chili relish

meatballs with marinara sauce

What kid doesn't enjoy spaghetti and meatballs? Well, this is a great way to get the kids eating whole grains without sacrificing flavor. Use lean ground beef or ground turkey in this recipe. For a faster meal, look for frozen store-bought meatballs—they aren't as tasty as homemade, but in a pinch, they work great.

makes: 16–20 small meatballs—enough for 6 meals, depending on serving size

1 8-ounce package cracked freekeh
   (1 cup dry, or about 2 cups cooked)
2½ cups vegetable broth
1 pound lean ground beef or ground turkey
2 cups jarred marinara sauce
½ medium onion, chopped fine
¼ cup Parmesan or Pecorino Romano
   cheese, grated
1 egg, slightly beaten

1 teaspoon oregano
1 teaspoon thyme
⅛ teaspoon crushed red pepper or a few
   cranks of fresh ground black pepper
½ teaspoon garlic powder
2 or 3 shakes of Worcestershire sauce (if you
   have it on hand)
olive oil
a dash of sea salt or Himalayan pink salt

Pour 2½ cups vegetable broth into a saucepan, add the freekeh, and bring to a boil for about 1 minute. Reduce heat to low. Cover and simmer for about 25 minutes until tender. Add 2 cups marinara sauce to the freekeh and simmer further for about 2 more minutes.

In a bowl, combine beaten egg, ground beef, spices, and cheese. Mix all ingredients with hands and form 1-inch size meatballs with the palms of your hands. Place on a plate and continue to make balls until the mixture is all gone.

In a large skillet, drizzle about 3 tablespoons of olive oil and heat up over medium heat. Carefully add meatballs to skillet and cook on one side until brown—about 1 or 2 minutes. Turn them to cook on all sides until they are brown and cooked through. Once done, gently remove with a slotted spoon and toss them in with the freekeh and sauce. Serve with a sprinkle of cheese.

note: if you have some freekeh and marinara left over, use it to stuff zucchini boats—see the recipe on page 76.

freekeh burger with chipotle mustard and yam fries

makes: 6–8 burgers

1 8-ounce package cracked freekeh
    (1 cup dry, or about 2 cups cooked)
2 eggs, beaten
1½ cups whole-wheat flour
½ onion, diced fine
1 cup chipotle mustard (or 2 chipotle peppers
    and 1 cup honey mustard blended together)
1 15-ounce can black beans, rinsed and drained
1 teaspoon apple cider vinegar

grapeseed or vegetable oil

spices:
1 tablespoon chili powder
2 tablespoons onion powder
2 teaspoons chipotle powder
1 teaspoon paprika (or smoked paprika!)
6 garlic cloves, chopped
sea salt to taste

Pour 2½ cups of water and the freekeh in a saucepan and bring to a boil for 1 minute. Reduce heat to low. Cover and simmer for about 25 minutes until the freekeh is tender. Once cooked, remove from heat and cool in refrigerator.

Pour spices in a large bowl and mix together. Add eggs, freekeh, black beans, chipotle mustard, onion, oil, vinegar, and 1 cup of the flour. Mix well.

Take a little of the leftover flour and pour on the counter. Take a small handful of the burger mixture and form a ball in your hands. Place the ball on the counter and slightly press into the flour on both sides so that there's a light dusting of flour on each side. Continue forming burgers. If hands become too sticky, coat your hands with a little flour in between forming the burgers.

In a nonstick skillet, heat up about ⅛-inch of grapeseed or vegetable oil on medium to high. Carefully place each burger into the heated oil. Cook on one side for about 3 to 4 minutes or until you begin to see the edges brown and crisp. Carefully flip the burger over and cook another 3 to 4 minutes. Cook only a few burgers at a time so you have room to flip them. Serve with chipotle mustard, lettuce, and onion.

yam fries

To make yam fries or sweet potato fries, simply scrub and rinse yams, leaving skins on if you wish. Slice lengthwise into narrow slices. Toss them into a bowl and drizzle with a little olive oil. Add a generous portion of chipotle powder, paprika, onion powder, garlic powder (not garlic salt), and a little salt. Mix to coat evenly. Place on a baking sheet lined with either tin foil or parchment paper. Bake at 350° for about 30 minutes or until they are fork-tender. Enjoy them hot or cold!

vegetarian empanadas

preheat oven: 375°
makes: 8–10 empanadas

for filling:
1 8-ounce package cracked freekeh
   (1 cup dry, or about 2 cups cooked)
2½ cups water or vegetable broth
½ of 14.5-ounce can black beans, drained
   and rinsed
2 tablespoons tomato paste
1 medium onion, diced
6 garlic cloves, diced
1 sweet red pepper, diced
2–4 tablespoons extra virgin olive oil

1 teaspoon cumin
2 tablespoons chili powder
2 tablespoons fajita or taco seasoning

for empanada dough:
2 cups unbleached whole-wheat flour
2 eggs
1 tablespoon vinegar
1 cup water
½ cup Earth Balance® or butter, softened
2 tablespoons olive oil

In a bowl, mix 1 beaten egg, vinegar, and water. Add the whole-wheat flour and the softened Earth Balance®. Using your fingers or a pastry cutter, blend the ingredients until the dough is moist and crumbly. Form into a ball and dust with a little flour. Place in a clean bowl, cover with plastic wrap, and chill in the fridge for at least an hour.

Pour 2½ cups of broth and the freekeh in a saucepan and bring to a boil, cooking for 1 minute. Reduce heat to low. Cover and simmer for about 25 minutes.

In a skillet on medium heat, drizzle a little olive oil and sauté diced onion, pepper, and garlic for about 5 minutes. Add in seasonings, tomato paste, beans, and cooked freekeh. Stir and remove from heat.

Remove dough from refrigerator and divide into two balls. On a floured surface, knead the dough slightly. Using a rolling pin, roll out dough into an ⅛-inch thick layer. Cut circles into the dough using a round cookie or biscuit cutter.

Spoon the filling onto one side of the circle. Fold over and crimp the edge shut with the back of a fork. Place each empanada on a greased cookie sheet. Whisk second egg and use a pastry brush to coat empanadas with it. Bake for 8–10 minutes or until golden brown.

freekeh pizza for kids!

preheat oven: 500°–525°
makes: 3 9-inch round thin-crust pizzas

for the crust:
1 envelope Fleischmann's Pizza Crust Yeast®
   (this kind works the best)
1¾ to 2 cups freekeh flour
1 teaspoon salt
⅔ cup very warm water
½ teaspoon garlic, dried or granulated
5 tablespoons good-quality olive oil
1 teaspoon coconut palm sugar or other
   granulated sugar

topping options:
use any kinds you enjoy!
use any kind of pizza sauce, or Arabiatta
   marinara sauce (it's a spicier kind of
   marinara sauce)
shredded mozzerella cheese
Parmesan cheese
fresh basil, dried Italian spices
a few shakes of red pepper flakes
black olives, onions, broccoli

In a small cup or bowl, add the warm water, packet of yeast, and sugar. Mix with a spoon and allow to sit undisturbed for about a minute.

Then transfer liquid to a large bowl and add about 1 cup of the flour, mixing well with a large spoon. Once blended, begin adding a little more of the flour, garlic, salt, and olive oil until ingredients are incorporated well. The mixture will be sticky.

Using your hands, transfer the dough to a floured surface and knead the dough for about 3–4 minutes until it becomes more elastic. Divide dough into 3 balls.

Transfer one of the balls to a baking sheet lined with parchment paper. Roll out the dough while on the paper until it becomes very thin. With your fingers, create an edge of dough to hold in the sauce. Repeat to make 3 pizzas.

Precook the pizza dough for about 10–12 minutes in a preheated oven on the lower rack. Once the edges of the pizza become golden brown, remove the pizza and add your sauce and desired toppings. Place back in oven, and cook for about another 10 minutes, or until the cheese begins to melt.

Sprinkle with a little more Parmesan cheese or red chili flakes and serve immediately.

bento box with meatloaf

"Bento box" is a common container meal in Japanese cuisine. It usually consists of meat, rice, and vegetables in a container that is easily transportable. Often, folks will make a "character bento" box called Kyraben that consists of video game or anime characters— made entirely of edible ingredients!

Have fun making something special for your child's lunch using fruits, veggies, and all kinds of things from the fridge! Use a Tupperware® container or a leftover carryout meal tray with a lid. Or if you want a more elaborate container, look for a real bento box—they come in laminated wood, bamboo, plastic, and metal containers. It would make a great birthday present and may be a fun way to get your child to try a variety of foods! Shop for them online or at your local Asian market.

In this recipe, I'm sneaking spinach and freekeh into the meatloaf!

preheat oven: 400°
makes: 1 loaf

1 pound lean ground beef
1 8-ounce package cracked freekeh
    (1 cup dry, or about 2 cups cooked)
2½ cups beef broth, or vegetable broth
½ cup ketchup
¾ cup tomato sauce (or use extra ketchup)
½ teaspoon salt
½ teaspoon pepper
⅛ teaspoon crushed red pepper flakes
2 eggs, beaten
½ cup onion, diced fine, any kind
1 tablespoon oregano (I used dried)

1 tablespoon prepared mustard
4 shakes of garlic powder
4 shakes of Worcestershire sauce (if you don't
    have any, skip it)
1 cup chopped frozen spinach, thawed and
    pressed to remove excess water (I prefer
    working with a bag instead of a box of
    frozen spinach)

for topping:
about ¼ cup ketchup
1 teaspoon prepared mustard

Pour 2½ cups of broth and the freekeh in a large saucepan and bring to a boil for 1 minute. Reduce heat to low. Cover and simmer for about 25 minutes until the freekeh is tender.

While the freekeh is cooking, prepare the other ingredients. In a large bowl, combine all ingredients and mix thoroughly. Once freekeh is cooked, add and mix again.

Line a casserole dish with foil and press beef mixture into a loaf-like shape in the middle of the pan. Make sure edges are packed firm. In a separate small bowl, mix the topping, then spread it evenly over the loaf.

Bake in preheated oven for about 1½ hours or until done.

Drain excess fat from the bottom of the pan, if any remains. Allow to rest a few minutes prior to slicing.

Have fun using sliced fruit, wedges of cheese, and other ingredients to make a bird or other animal!

chapter 4

stand-alone sides

summer salads and
savory sides

curried freekeh salad

I am a huge fan of WYPR and have donated illustrations for their T-shirts and other giveaways for their on-air fundraisers over the years. But one year, I donated a bunch of yummy lunch to the staff and their volunteers. This salad was a big hit with them.

preheat oven: 375°
makes: 6 servings

1 8-ounce package cracked freekeh
   (1 cup dry, or about 2 cups cooked)
2½ cups vegetable broth
1 sweet potato
1 large red pepper, diced
½ red onion, diced
4 garlic cloves, diced

2 tablespoons olive oil
3 to 4 tablespoons mild curry powder
½ cup dried cranberries or raisins
1 cup dried apricots, chopped
1 cup peas, frozen and thawed
1 cup sliced almonds or pepita seeds
salt and pepper to taste

Pour 2½ cups of broth and the freekeh in a saucepan and bring to a boil for 1 minute. Reduce heat to low. Cover and simmer for about 25 minutes until the freekeh is tender. Once the freekeh is cooked, place in a separate dish to cool in the refrigerator.

Scrub the sweet potato and cut into 1-inch cubes. Place sweet potatoes on a foil-lined baking sheet and drizzle a little olive oil on them. Cover with tin foil, and bake in a 375° oven for about 25 minutes or until tender. Remove from oven and set aside.

In a large skillet, heat up oil over medium heat and toss in red peppers, onions, and garlic. Cook for 3–5 minutes, then toss in curry powder, salt, and pepper. Cook further until the onions are translucent. Set aside to cool. Toss freekeh in a bowl with vegetable mixture, and add dried fruits, nuts, peas, and sweet potatoes. Season to taste and serve.

optional: for variations, add sauteed cauliflower, chickpeas, or lentils. You can look for purple sweet potatoes as shown in the photo!

lentil salad with sugar snap peas, tomatoes, and freekeh

I created this when I was the demo gal at Trader Joe's. So many of my customers asked me what they could use the store's fully cooked lentils with—so one summer I came up with this recipe that featured lentils. You can find fully cooked, vacuum-packed lentils in the produce sections of many grocery stores. They are often near the herbs and refrigerated salsas.

makes: 6-8 servings

1 8-ounce package cracked freekeh
    (1 cup dry, or about 2 cups cooked)
2½ cups water
½ pound fresh sugar snap peas, cut in half
12-ounce package grape tomatoes, sliced
    in half

4 ounces crumbled nonfat feta or goat cheese
1 package fully cooked lentils (about 2 cups)
¼ cup red wine vinaigrette or a low-sodium
    Italian dressing
fresh cracked pepper and salt to taste

Pour water and the freekeh in a saucepan and bring to a boil for 1 minute. Reduce heat to low. Cover and simmer for about 25 minutes until the freekeh is tender. Once cooked, remove from heat and cool in refrigerator. When freekeh is cool, toss in a large bowl with all ingredients except for the cheese. Stir gently so it doesn't become mushy. Add plenty of fresh cracked pepper. Gently stir in cheese.

timesaver option: if you cook up freekeh and keep some in the freezer, you can thaw it out and make this salad in about 5 minutes. I've seen fully cooked lentils in a vacuum-packed container in the produce department. I use half a bag of these for this recipe and freeze the rest to toss in soup.

summer salad with heirloom tomatoes, goat cheese, and basil

Because heirloom tomatoes are grown from non-hybridized seeds, they are packed full of more flavor and often have less acid. Of course you can use any tomatoes in this recipe, but look for heirlooms and you will be in for a treat! Look for the crazy green-striped ones, dark green, and even bright yellow!

Better yet, grow your own next spring! Look at your local nursery for seedlings or find seeds online at: www.tomatobob.com.

A lot of folks I talk with have never eaten sugar snap peas. They are sweet and crunchy and are also delicious with hummus instead of crackers!

Fully cooked freekeh, chilled

fresh heirloom tomatoes, diced in bite-sized pieces

goat cheese, crumbled (or switch it up and use feta another day)

fresh basil

fresh sugar snap peas (hull and all!)

red wine vinaigrette and extra virgin olive oil, or Italian dressing (don't get one that is too salty)

cracked pepper, sea salt, or Himalayan pink salt

Simply mix ingredients above, taste-test, and add more seasoning if necessary.

Overrun with greens from the garden? Add this salad on top of a hearty plateful and grill up some chicken on the side!

roasted beet salad with cannellini beans, pistachios, and feta

Did you know that health experts say that cannellini beans contain twice as much iron as beef? Plus beans are loaded with lean protein and fiber and are deeelish.

For this salad, you don't have to measure precisely—add as much or as little of the ingredients as you like.

preheat oven: 375°
makes: 6 servings

1 8-ounce package cracked freekeh (1 cup dry, or about 2 cups cooked)
2½ cups vegetable broth
a few tablespoons olive oil
about ½ cup crumbled nonfat feta cheese or nonfat goat cheese
1 15.5-ounce can of cannellini beans, rinsed and drained

2–3 cups of fresh beets, scrubbed, skins on and diced (about 6–8 beets)
a few teaspoons apple cider vinegar
pistachio nuts or pepita seeds (green pumpkin seeds)
sea salt and cracked pepper to taste
fresh diced mint or chopped fresh basil (optional)

optional: toss in fresh chopped spring onion or Italian parsley.

Preheat the oven to 375°. Place beets on a foil-covered baking sheet. Drizzle a little olive oil on top and bake on the middle rack in the preheated oven. Cook for about 30 minutes or until tender. Remove from oven and let cool to room temperature.

Pour 2½ cups of broth and the freekeh in a saucepan and bring to a boil, cooking for 1 minute. Reduce heat to low. Cover and simmer for about 25 minutes until the freekeh is tender. Let the freekeh cool before making the salad.

Toss ingredients together. Add the crumbled cheese. Serve chilled.

optional: serve the salad on top of arugula or other greens drizzled with a little apple cider vinegar and olive oil.

Greek-style freekeh with Kalamata olives and tomatoes

Use cherry tomatoes, Little Splenditos® or grape tomatoes for this salad. They are sweet and more firm than larger tomatoes.

If you have some leftover rotisserie chicken, dice it up and toss into this recipe for lunch the next day.

makes: 4-6 servings

1 8-ounce package cracked freekeh
    (1 cup dry, or about 2 cups cooked)
2½ cups water or chicken broth
fresh tomatoes, cut into chunks (I really like
    grape tomatoes cut in half for this because
    they're so sweet)
Kalamata olives, pitted and cut

fresh basil leaves, a good handful or two,
    chopped
2 tablespoons extra virgin olive oil
a few tablespoons red wine vinegar
plenty of fresh cracked pepper and salt
    to taste
low-fat crumbled feta cheese or crumbled
    goat cheese

Pour 2½ cups of water or broth and the freekeh in a saucepan and bring to a boil for 1 minute. Reduce heat to low. Cover and simmer for about 25 minutes until the freekeh is tender. After it's cooked, remove from heat and let cool in the refrigerator. Slice tomatoes and olives. Toss in a large bowl with the freekeh. Add olive oil, red wine vinegar, and the remaining ingredients, and stir.

optional: instead of olive oil and red wine vinegar, try one of these favorite premade dressings: Newman's Own Greek Vinaigrette Dressing® or Trader Joe's Organic Red Wine & Olive Oil Vinaigrette®.

tabbouleh

Try this also in a wrap with hummus—check out page 52.

makes: 6–8 servings

1 8-ounce package cracked freekeh
    (1 cup dry, or about 2 cups cooked)
2½ cups water or vegetable broth
2 cups flat-leaf parsley
½ cup fresh mint, chopped
grape tomatoes, diced (I used Little Splenditos
    from Trader Joe's)

½ cup seedless cucumber, diced
3–4 tablespoons fresh lemon juice
3–4 garlic cloves, diced (or 3 teaspoons
    chopped from jar)
salt and pepper to taste
extra virgin olive oil

Pour water or broth and the freekeh in a saucepan and bring to a boil, cooking for 1 minute. Reduce heat to low. Cover and simmer for about 25 minutes until the freekeh is tender. Once cooked, remove from heat and set aside to cool.

Dice the tomatoes, cucumbers, and garlic. Add all ingredients in a large bowl and mix well with a spoon. Taste and adjust seasoning if needed.

warm freekeh with peas, coconut oil, and Himalayan pink salt

My foodie friend, Katrina, made this one up, and it's so simple and good! Coconut oil's all the rage for being one of the "good fats" for fighting fat. Plus it has a lot of nutrients and tastes delicious! And it can be heated at a higher temperature than olive oil, so it works great for recipes like the banana pancakes on page 34 to make nice crispy edges on pancakes or pan-fried fish.

makes: 6-8 servings

1 8-ounce package cracked freekeh
    (1 cup dry, or about 2 cups cooked)
2½ cups vegetable broth
1 small bag of frozen sweet peas (or baby
    frozen peas)

2–3 tablespoons coconut oil
Himalayan pink salt (or any kind of good
    Kosher or sea salt)

Pour vegetable broth and the freekeh in a saucepan and bring to a boil, cooking for 1 minute. Reduce heat to low. Add in coconut oil. Cover and simmer for about 20 minutes until the freekeh is tender. Add the frozen peas and cook further for about 5 more minutes. Season with fresh cracked Himalayan pink salt and serve.

stuffed heirloom tomatoes

Heirloom tomatoes, often called "ugly" tomatoes because of their unusual shapes, are perhaps the most flavorful of all tomatoes! They are grown from heirloom varieties that have not been bred for their perfect color or size for stores. So they have retained their delicious flavors! Look for them at your local farmer's markets and healthy grocery stores.

This recipe is adapted from Katerina at Diethood.com.

I'm using some leftover freekeh that's been cooked in vegetable broth in this recipe.

preheat oven: 375°
makes: 6 large heirloom tomatoes or 8 medium

6 large heirloom tomatoes
1 cup fully cooked freekeh
2 teaspoons tarragon, dried or fresh
2½ cups chopped frozen spinach, thawed
¾ cup pine nuts or walnuts

2–3 garlic cloves, minced fine
a little drizzle of walnut or extra virgin olive oil
¾ cup Parmesan cheese (or add a little Asiago cheese as well!)
freshly ground pepper and sea salt to taste

Thaw chopped frozen spinach and press out extra liquid. Mix freekeh, tarragon, spinach, nuts, garlic, and cheese in a large bowl, stirring to combine. Drizzle in olive oil or walnut oil.

For the tomatoes, cut out the main part of the core with a sharp knife to allow room for the filling. Use a small spoon to scoop out a little more tomato to make more room if necessary. Fill the tomatoes with the vegetable mixture and pack them generously.

Place the tomatoes in a 9x12-inch inch baking dish lined with parchment paper. Add about ⅛ inch of water to the pan. Cover lightly with a piece of foil. Bake for about 30 minutes. Remove foil, add a little more cheese to the tops, and bake further until the skin of the tomatoes begins to split slightly and the cheese begins to melt.

arugula salad with figs, marcona almonds, goat cheese, and balsamic glaze

Arugula greens have a nice peppery taste that is a welcome change to the old hum-drum spring mix. They work great with the sweetness of the balsamic glaze and marcona almonds in this recipe. Marcona almonds are a rare treat since they are a tad bit more expensive—but well worth it! They have a unique creamy taste that is different from traditional almonds.

cooked cold freekeh (cooked in vegetable broth)

arugula greens

fresh ripe figs, quartered, skins on

marcona almonds

good-quality goat cheese (I used plain but have used honey goat cheese, too)

balsamic glaze (not vinegar)

a little fresh cracked pepper and sea salt or Himalayan pink salt

Simply toss the above ingredients together and drizzle with balsamic glaze.

Serve room temperature or chilled.

zucchini and broccoli salad with freekeh and tahini ginger dressing

Tahini is made from sesame seeds and has a rich, fantastic flavor. It works great with all kinds of dressings and is one of the ingredients in homemade hummus! For variations of this salad, change up the vegetables and use whatever seasonal ingredients you have. Try adding in shredded carrots, raisins, and shredded purple cabbage, and you have it a whole new way!

makes: 4-6 servings

salad:
about 1½–2 cups cooked freekeh, cooled
2 cups fresh broccoli crowns
1 medium zucchini, diced, raw
cracked pepper and a little salt to taste

dressing (makes enough to top a nice green salad another day):
2 tablespoons tahini (look for this in a glass jar or tin can in the gourmet, International, or vinegar area in the store)

3–4 tablespoons rice vinegar or red wine vinegar
2–3 cloves of garlic
½ teaspoon fresh minced ginger (or look for ginger in a tube in the refrigerated section)
2 tablespoons creamy peanut butter
1 tablespoon toasted sesame oil

In a food processor, mix all the dressing ingredients and taste-test. Dressing can be thickened by adding more tahini or peanut butter if desired.

Dice up the broccoli and place in a saucepan with about 1 inch of water or use a steamer. Only steam broccoli to soften slightly and to brighten the color—about 2 minutes. Once done, immediately remove from heat and drain water. Pour cold water over top to cool it down. Then drain liquid and pour the broccoli into a large bowl.

Add the diced vegetables to the cooked freekeh and mix with a spoon.

Add the dressing a little at a time and mix in with a spoon. Taste-test and serve chilled.

Mediterranean freekeh salad

makes: 6 servings

1 8-ounce package cracked freekeh
   (1 cup dry, or about 2 cups cooked)
2½ cups water or vegetable broth
1½ cups pitted Kalamata olives or French
   herbed black olives
1½ cups or more fire-roasted tomatoes
   or sun-dried tomatoes packed in herbed
   olive oil

2–4 garlic cloves, crushed
1½ cups fresh basil leaves, chopped
handful pine nuts
3 teaspoons freshly squeezed lemon juice
about 1½ cups of pearled fresh mozzarella
   balls
fresh cracked pepper, sea salt, and additional
   oregano to taste

note: retain some of the olive oil from the tomatoes to add to this dish.

optional: add garbanzo or cannellini beans, or get a rotisserie chicken and serve on the side.

Pour 2½ cups of water or broth and the freekeh in a saucepan and bring to a boil for 1 minute. Reduce heat to low. Cover and simmer for about 25 minutes until the freekeh is tender. Once the freekeh is cooked, place in a separate dish to cool in the refrigerator.

While the freekeh is cooling, cut olives in half, along with the tomatoes and basil. In a small skillet, drizzle a little extra virgin olive oil and heat up on medium. Toss in the pine nuts and cook them carefully until golden, swirling the pan above the heat source, so they don't burn. Remove from heat when done, and set aside to cool.

Once the freekeh is fully cooled, add ingredients except for the cheese, and mix gently with a spoon. Drizzle in some of the remaining olive oil that came with the tomatoes. Taste-test and season to taste. Lastly, stir in the cheese, being careful not to mash it.

Serve room temperature or chilled.

note: using fresh basil, fresh-squeezed lemon juice, and fresh garlic are essential to the bright flavor in this dish. If you cannot locate pearled mozzarella, look for other fresh mozzarella that you can dice up into smaller chunks. For a really special treat, use diced buffalo mozzerella cheese!

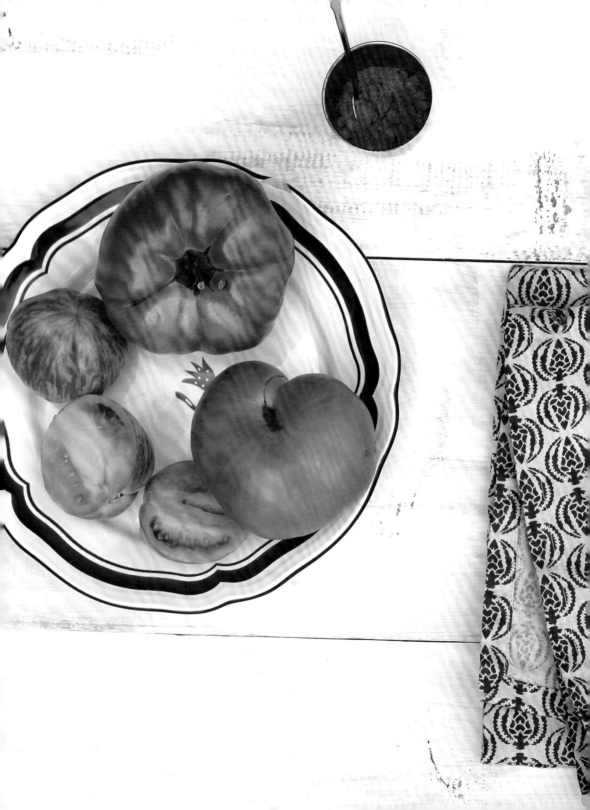

chapter 5

sunday soirée

festive ways to prepare freekeh
and share with your friends

sweet and savory Middle Eastern beef

Tastes even bettter on day 2!

preheat oven: 375°
makes: 4-6 servings

½ cup of freekeh, uncooked
1½ cups beef broth or water
1¼ pounds of beef (I used round cut)
1½ teaspoons allspice, ground
½ teaspoon cinnamon, ground
3 cloves of garlic, minced fine

¼ to ½ cup pistachios, pine nuts, or slivered
   almonds
extra virgin olive oil
a little fresh mint, chopped (optional)
2 small or 1 large sweet potato or yam,
   diced and roasted (I leave the skins on)
salt and pepper to taste

Preheat the oven to 375°. Toss the sweet potatoes in a little olive oil. Place on a baking sheet lined with parchment paper (if you have it). Cover lightly with foil and cook for about 25 minutes or until fork tender. Once done, remove and set aside.

Dice the beef in small, bite-sized pieces. Drizzle a little olive oil in a large skillet and heat up over medium heat. Place meat pieces in skillet and cook until browned on all sides, about 4–6 minutes. Add in the spices, broth, and freekeh, and raise heat to high. Bring to a boil, reduce heat, and cover. Allow to simmer for about 25 minutes or until freekeh is tender. Once the liquid is evaporated and the freekeh is tender, add salt and pepper to taste. Add the sweet potatoes and nuts and top with mint.

Serve immediately!

meatloaf with spinach and freekeh

Leftovers can be used for making bento box edible art for kids! See page 88 for some fun ideas. This recipe is a great way to add more greens into your meal.

preheat oven: 400°
makes: 4-6 servings

1 8-ounce package cracked freekeh
   (1 cup dry, or about 2 cups cooked)
2½ cups water or beef broth
1 pound of lean ground beef or ground turkey
½ cup ketchup, plus a little extra for topping
¾ cup tomato sauce (or just add extra
   ketchup)
½ teaspoon salt
few shakes of black pepper and crushed red
   pepper flakes

2 eggs, beaten
½ cup onion, diced fine
1 cup frozen spinach, thawed and drained
1 tablespoon oregano
1 teaspoon prepared mustard
4 shakes garlic powder
4 shakes of Worcestershire sauce (optional)

topping:
about ¼ cup ketchup or more if desired

Pour water or broth and the freekeh in a saucepan and bring to a boil, cooking for 1 minute. Reduce heat to low. Add in the garlic. Cover and simmer for about 25 minutes until the freekeh is tender. Once cooked, remove from heat. Let stand to cool a few minutes before the next step.

In a large bowl, add all ingredients including the fully cooked freekeh. Mix thoroughly with your hands. Line a casserole dish with foil, or spray with cooking spray. Add beef mixture and press into a loaf shape. Top with a little more ketchup and coat. Bake in preheated oven for about 1 hour and 15 minutes or until done. Once done, drain any remaining fat from pan. Let meatloaf rest about 5 minutes before cutting.

30-minute paella

There are really no limits to the ways you can prepare paella! One thing not to compromise on, however, is the quality of the seafood for this recipe. Look for fresh, wild-caught shrimp—they have better flavor. Add in chunks of cod, mussels, or scallops for variations.

makes: 4–6 servings

1 pack (6 links) spicy Andouille sausage, diced and browned
extra virgin olive oil
1 sweet red or yellow pepper, diced
1 green pepper, diced
10 garlic cloves, diced
1 large onion, diced fine
1 large fresh tomato, diced fine
1 8-ounce package cracked freekeh
   (1 cup dry, or about 2 cups cooked)

2½ cups chicken broth, vegetable broth, or water
1 10.5-ounce can of clam sauce
1 cup fresh or frozen peas, thawed
14–18 medium to large shrimp, shelled, deveined, and rinsed
¾ teaspoon saffron
cayenne pepper, to taste
salt and plenty of fresh cracked pepper to taste
few sprigs fresh parsley
lemon wedges

Drizzle a little olive oil in a large skillet and heat up on medium. Toss in diced sausage and brown on all sides for about 5 minutes. Once cooked, remove sausage and set aside. Keeping the browned bits in the same skillet, add diced onions, peppers, and garlic. Cook on medium heat until tender. Add a little more olive oil if desired. Toss in diced tomato and the spices, and cook for about 1 more minute. Add freekeh to skillet and stir thoroughly. Add the cooked sausage, clam sauce, broth, and peas. Cover and reduce heat to simmer. Cook for an additional 20 minutes or until the freekeh is tender and the liquid has been absorbed. Add the shrimp and cook for a few more minutes (about 6) until pink. Garnish with fresh chopped parsley and lemon and serve.

optional: add fresh mussels, clams, or scallops when adding shrimp.

Persian stuffed chicken

I cook my chicken in a roasting bag, and it always turns out great! Serve the whole chicken on a platter, or cut up the pieces and place on top of stuffing as shown.

preheat oven: 350°
makes: 6 servings

1 whole chicken with organs removed and
  cavity emptied
1 8-ounce package cracked freekeh
  (1 cup dry, or about 2 cups cooked)
2½ cups chicken broth or vegetable broth, plus
  ½ cup for the stuffing
½ cup dried apricots, cut in half
½ cup pistachios, chopped coarsely (or use
  slivered almonds)
6–8 prunes, cut in half
1 carrot, diced

1 medium onion, diced (about a cup)
1–2 teaspoons cinnamon
a little olive oil
1 teaspoon cumin
1 teaspoon coriander
a few cranks of black pepper
about 4–6 strips of lemon peel (about ¼-inch
  wide strips of lemon)
about 2–3 teaspoons of sea salt or Kosher salt
1 tablespoon ketchup or tomato paste

Pour 2½ cups of chicken broth in a saucepan, add the freekeh, and bring to a boil, cooking for 1 minute. Reduce heat to low. Cover and simmer for about 25 minutes until tender.

While the freekeh is cooking, rinse the chicken in cold water. In a small bowl, mix about 2–3 tablespoons of olive oil, 1 teaspoon of cinnamon, and about a teaspoon of salt. Apply mixture to the outside of the chicken, rubbing it into the skin. Rinse hands thoroughly and set chicken in a large bowl in the refrigerator while the freekeh is cooking.

In a saucepan, add the cumin, coriander, and cinnamon with a little olive oil. Heat spices over medium heat for about 45 seconds, then add the diced onion and cook until the onions are transparent. Add about ½ cup of chicken broth or water to the skillet. Add lemon peel, ketchup, and the diced carrot, and cook for another 2–3 minutes, then set aside.

Once the freekeh is cooked, mix the carrots and onion mixture with the freekeh and add in the lemon peel, apricots, prunes, and pistachios. Mix thoroughly with a spoon. Add about a teaspoon of salt and some fresh cracked pepper. Bring out the chicken from the refrigerator and place it in a roasting bag with the open end facing the back of the chicken. Place the chicken breast-side up in a shallow roasting pan. With a large spoon, begin to fill the cavity of the chicken with the freekeh stuffing mixture until it's full. With a piece of twine or string, tie the

2 drumstick legs together. If there is remaining stuffing, place it in the bottom of the bag with a little water. Poke a small steam hole in the roasting bag. Tie the roasting bag with the tie, and place in preheated oven for about an hour. Feel free to baste the chicken with the juices a few times during cooking.

The chicken is done when it is no longer pink against the bone. Once cooked, remove it from the oven, and allow it to cool off on top of the stove for about 5–7 minutes. Remove from the bag and either place whole on a platter to serve, or remove the stuffing from the chicken and serve the cut-up chicken on top of the stuffing as shown in the photo below.

freekeh-stuffed peppers

You can save time with this recipe if you have leftover freekeh from making freekeh tacos! Or make the freekeh portion of this recipe the night before and stuff them the next day.

preheat oven: 350°
makes: 6 servings

1 8-ounce package cracked freekeh
   (1 cup dry, or about 2 cups cooked)
2½ cups vegetable broth
4–6 sweet peppers, sliced in half and seeds
   removed
1 15-ounce can aduki beans or pinto beans
1 12-ounce jar of your favorite salsa
2 tablespoons tomato paste or ketchup
6–8 cloves of garlic, chopped

1 small onion, diced
2 limes, juiced
½ bunch of fresh cilantro
1½ cups corn, fresh or frozen, thawed
2 cups grape tomatoes, sliced in half
salt and fresh cracked pepper to taste
2 teaspoons chipotle powder
1 avocado, diced
topping option: shredded cheese

Add about 2 inches of water to a large pot and bring to a boil. Reduce heat to low and add in the sweet peppers. Cover and cook for about 4–5 minutes until they're slightly soft. Remove peppers from pot and set aside to cool.

Pour 2½ cups broth and the freekeh in a saucepan and bring to a boil for about a minute. Reduce heat to medium. Stir in tomato paste, onion, chipotle powder, and garlic. Cover and simmer for about 25 minutes until the freekeh is tender. In a large bowl, combine freekeh with remaining ingredients except the steamed peppers, stir, and set aside.

Place the peppers in a 9x12-inch casserole dish. With a large spoon, carefully fill the peppers with freekeh mixture. The contents can come up above the edge of the pepper. Pour about ¼ inch of water in the dish and place in preheated oven. Cook for about 30 minutes.

optional: if you are topping peppers with grated cheese, add cheese after the peppers have been in the oven for about 20 minutes. Sprinkle cheese on and cook for another 10 minutes.

jambalaya with shrimp and andouille sausage

As always, you can make it your own by adding more or less of the ingredients listed here. If you know me by now, you know I like my foods super-spicy, so watch out!

makes: 6 servings

1 package (6 links) chipotle or Andouille sausage, diced and browned

2–3 large sweet peppers, diced

1 large onion, diced

10 garlic cloves, diced (I know, I know, just go for it!)

1 14.5-ounce can diced fire-roasted tomatoes (including liquid)

1 8-ounce package cracked freekeh (1 cup dry, or about 2 cups cooked)

2½ cups vegetable broth

4 tablespoons olive oil

¼ teaspoon cayenne pepper (or less if you're afraid!)

1 tablespoon Cholula Hot Sauce® or any kind of hot sauce you enjoy

¼ teaspoon paprika

¼ teaspoon cumin

1 tablespoon chili powder

¼ teaspoon celery seeds

10–12 large shrimp, peeled, deveined, and rinsed

salt and pepper to taste

garnish with chopped cilantro or parsley

In a large skillet, heat oil over medium heat. Add diced sausage and brown, making sure it's cooked through. Remove sausage from heat and set aside. In same skillet, add a little more oil and toss in peppers, onion, garlic, and spices, cooking on medium heat for about 5 minutes or until onions are translucent. Add uncooked freekeh, tomatoes, and broth and stir. Reduce heat to low and add sausage back into the skillet. Cover and simmer for 15–20 minutes. After about 20 minutes, stir, add raw shrimp to the skillet, and cover. Cook another 5–7 minutes. Add a little more water, if necessary. Once the shrimp is pink and firm, the dish is complete. Serve with freshly squeezed lemon or lime juice and chopped cilantro.

Moroccan lamb with dried fruits and nuts

This recipe is inspired by my late brother, Larry's, Moroccan lamb tagine.

preheat oven: 325°
makes: 4 servings

1 8-ounce package cracked freekeh
   (1 cup dry, or about 2 cups cooked)
2 pounds lean lamb stew meat, or shoulder
   meat, cubed
1 lemon, juiced and grated for zest
1 tablespoon olive oil
1 onion, chopped
4 carrots, diced
6 garlic cloves, chopped
1–2 cinnamon sticks

1 teaspoon honey
2 teaspoons cumin
1 teaspoon ginger
1 teaspoon tomato paste
3 cups beef or vegetable broth
20 prunes, pitted, sliced in half
10 dried apricots, pitted, sliced in half
¼ cup chopped pistachios or almonds
10–15 fresh mint leaves

On the stove, heat up olive oil in a flameproof, oven-safe pot on medium to high heat. Add lamb and sear until browned. Stir often. Reduce heat. Remove lamb and set aside. Scrape any browned bits of meat in the bottom of the pot. Toss in onion and garlic and cook about 5 minutes until soft. Add lamb back in with the onions. Add lemon juice and zest, broth, cumin, ginger, tomato paste, cinnamon sticks, and honey and stir. Add in freekeh, apricots, prunes, carrots, and mint. Turn heat off and cover. Remove from stove and put in preheated oven on the middle rack for 1 hour 15 minutes. Stir after 1 hour. Add ½ cup of water or broth if it appears too dry. Place lid back on and cook for an additional 15–30 minutes. Remove from the oven and toss in pistachios or almonds. Serve immediately.

optional: to make this even more authentically Moroccan, use 3–4 slices of preserved lemon. Add 2–3 thin strips of lemon peel into the pot when you add in the carrots.

Preserved lemon can be found in a jar in the international or gourmet sections of many grocery stores.

freekeh-stuffed portobello mushrooms

I volunteer with Dr. Oz's nonprofit, HealthCorps, and we selected this recipe to serve at the Grassroots Gala Fundraiser in 2013. It was a big hit! The caterer made it with small mushrooms as an hors d'oeuvre.

preheat oven: 375°
makes: 8-10 servings

1 8-ounce package cracked freekeh
   (1 cup dry, or about 2 cups cooked)
2½ cups vegetable broth
1 medium onion, diced
1 red pepper, diced
4 tablespoons butter or extra virgin olive oil
½ cup cooking sherry
1 cup fresh spinach, chopped and stems
   removed

1 cup Parmesan cheese, grated
1 egg, beaten
8–10 large portobello mushrooms
(or if you are making them as an hors d'oeuvre,
   use 25–30 cremini mushrooms)
2 teaspoons thyme
1 tablespoon onion powder
1 tablespoon garlic powder
salt and fresh black pepper to taste

Pour 2½ cups of broth in a saucepan, add the freekeh, and bring to a boil, cooking for 1 minute. Reduce heat to low. Cover and simmer for about 25 minutes.

Preheat oven to 375°.

Rinse mushrooms and separate the caps from the stems. Pat the mushroom caps dry with a paper towel and set aside. Dice stems and set aside.

Add butter or oil, onion, red pepper, diced mushroom stems, and dry seasonings to a large skillet. Cook over medium heat for about 5 minutes or until ingredients are tender. Add spinach and sherry and cook for another 2–4 minutes. Continue to cook spinach until it's wilted and reduced in volume. Turn off heat. Transfer from the skillet and place in a large bowl. Add the freekeh, cheese, and egg to the large bowl.

Drizzle a little olive oil on both sides of the mushroom caps and place on a foil-lined baking sheet. Stuff each mushroom cap, packing firmly. Bake in preheated oven for about 20–25 minutes.

optional: for a variation, add in diced bits of sausage that have been browned in a skillet. Toss in when you add in the cooked freekeh. Try mixing in a little grated Asiago cheese.

salmon with freekeh, cabbage, and sugar snap peas

Wild-caught salmon is rich in flavor and is a good source of omega-3s. It has so much flavor on its own–you really don't need to do much to it to prepare it!

preheat oven: 400°
makes: 2–3 servings, depending on the size of filet

for the marinade:
¼ cup low-sodium soy sauce
1 tablespoon fish sauce (optional)
1–2 teaspoons dried or fresh grated ginger
sea salt and fresh cracked pepper to taste
cayenne pepper or white pepper

1 8-ounce package cracked freekeh
   (1 cup dry, or about 2 cups cooked)
2½ cups chicken broth

1 pound filet of wild-caught salmon
(or ask your fishmonger to cut you 2 filets; one
   per person)
Hoisin sauce (for topping)

4–6 cloves garlic, chopped
about 1½ cups shredded cabbage
1½–2 cups sugar snap peas
1 small onion diced
12–14 shitake mushrooms, diced
toasted sesame seed oil

Take marinade ingredients and mix together in a bowl. Place the salmon filets in a shallow dish or ziploc bag with the marinade and place in refrigerator for at least an hour, or even overnight for more flavor.

Pour 2½ cups of broth and freekeh in a saucepan and bring to a boil, cooking for 1 minute. Reduce heat to low. Add in a drizzle of toasted sesame seed oil; then cover and simmer for about 25 minutes.

While freekeh is cooking, heat about 2 tablespoons of toasted sesame seed oil in a skillet over medium heat. Add onion, garlic, mushrooms, cabbage, and sugar snap peas. Cook for about 5–7 minutes or until onions are translucent, and set aside.

Place the salmon in a baking dish and place in preheated oven. Cook salmon for about 7 minutes on one side. Flip over and drizzle a little marinade over top and cook further for another 5-7 minutes or until done.

While salmon is in the oven go back to finishing the freekeh. Add the cooked freekeh to the skillet with the mushrooms and onion mixture. Cook on medium heat about 2–3 minutes, and set aside while you are finishing the salmon.

Place the freekeh on a plate and place salmon on top. Serve right away with a Hoisin sauce and enjoy immediately.

yam and spinach freekeh fritter

makes: 6–8 4-inch fritters

2 cups yams or sweet potatoes (about 2 medium-sized), cooked and mashed (I leave the skins on)

1 cup frozen chopped spinach, thawed and water pressed out of it (about half a bag of frozen chopped)

1 cup cooked freekeh (a little less than ½ cup before cooking)

½ cup almond meal or almond flour

1 teaspoon chipotle chili powder (or ½ teaspoon for milder flavor)

3 teaspoons cumin

¼ teaspoon paprika or smoked paprika

½ teaspoon sea salt or Kosher salt

1 medium onion,

6 garlic cloves, minced

2 teaspoons mild chili powder (more or less depending on your spice desire)

1 egg

a little cilantro (optional)

about 2 tablespoons lime juice (if you don't have it, skip it)

cooking oil: either olive oil, coconut oil, or grapeseed oil

Chop up the yams or sweet potatoes and either roast them with a little olive oil at 350° in the oven on a cookie sheet until tender (about 30 minutes), or boil them in water on top of the stove until tender. Once cooked, mash them and set aside. Place spinach in a large bowl and also set aside.

In a skillet, add a little olive oil and cook the onions over medium heat along with the chipotle chili powder, cumin, paprika, garlic, and mild chili powder. Cook for a few minutes, stirring often. Once onion is tender and translucent, remove from heat and set aside to cool briefly.

Once the onion and spices are cool, add them to the bowl with yams and spinach. Add in the fully cooked freekeh and raw egg. Stir ingredients until they are well blended.

With your hands, begin forming the fritters by placing some of the mixture in your palms and pressing it together. Make sure that the edges are fairly compact. Continue to form them until all the mixture is used, then place them on a plate.

To cook the fritters, pour cooking oil into a new skillet and heat up over medium-high heat. Add enough oil for about ⅛ inch high in the skillet. Be careful not to let it get too hot and smoky. Using two spatulas, carefully place each fritter one at a time in the hot oil, carefully so as not to splatter the hot oil. Add 2–3 to the skillet at a time but do not overcrowd so you can flip them easily. Cook each fritter for a few minutes until you see the edges of the fritter begin to get brown and crisp—about 4–5 minutes. Turn each fritter carefully over and continue to cook until golden brown on the other side. Once done, remove them and place on a plate lined with a paper towel to cool slightly.

Serve with a garnish of diced tomatoes, pico de gallo, or your favorite salsa. Top with a little queso fresco or crumbled goat cheese and a wedge of lime. For a little dipping sauce, make a dressing with plain nonfat Greek-style yogurt mixed with lime juice, a little fresh crushed garlic, and honey! Or look for Wallaby Passion Fruit Yogurt® or Noosa Mango Yoghurt® and add a little garlic to it.

great side options: look for corn chili relish at Trader Joe's or farmer's markets. Serve with pinto beans cooked with garlic.

freekeh pizza

I first learned how to make pizza back in high school in my gourmet foods class. They nicknamed me "Bonzerelli" because I used to make pizzas so often that I began to number them each time, trying to perfect the dough! I think I got up to about 53 pizzas by the time I finished college. It made me quite popular with the other art students, let me tell you! This pizza should be numbered about 58!

preheat oven: 500°–525°
makes: 3 9-inch round thin-crust pizzas

for the crust:

1 envelope Fleischmann's Pizza Crust Yeast® (this kind works the best)
1¾–2 cups freekeh flour
1 teaspoon salt
⅔ cup very warm water
½ teaspoon garlic, dried or granulated
5 tablespoons good-quality olive oil (or better yet, use garlic-infused olive oil)*

teaspoon of coconut palm sugar or other granulated sugar
topping options: use any kinds you enjoy!
any kind of pizza sauce, or Arabiatta marinara sauce (it's a spicier kind of marinara sauce)
shredded mozzarella cheese, buffalo mozzarella, or crumbled goat cheese
Parmesan cheese
a few shakes of red pepper flakes

In a small cup or bowl, add the warm water, packet of yeast, and sugar. Mix with a spoon and allow to sit undisturbed for about a minute.

Then transfer liquid to a large bowl and add in about 1 cup of the flour, mixing well with a large spoon. Once blended, begin adding a little more of the flour, garlic, salt, and olive oil until ingredients are incorporated well. The mixture will be sticky.

Using your hands, transfer the dough to a floured surface and knead the dough for about 3–4 minutes until it becomes more elastic. Divide dough into three balls.

Transfer one of the balls to a baking sheet lined with parchment paper. Roll out the dough while on the paper until it becomes very thin. With your fingers, create an edge of dough to hold in the sauce. Repeat to make 3 pizzas.

Precook the pizza dough for about 10–12 minutes in a preheated oven on the lower rack. Once the edges of the pizza become golden brown, remove the pizza and add your sauce and desired toppings. Place back in the oven, and cook further for about another 10 minutes or until the cheese begins to melt.

Sprinkle with a little more Parmesan cheese or red chili flakes and serve immediately.

*Make your own infused oil by simply placing a few cloves of garlic in a glass container with some olive oil. Cover with a foil lid and allow to season on the counter for a few hours prior to using. You can also keep this in the refrigerator for a few days to use in dressings.

stuffing with chicken apple sausage

A tasty, healthier whole-grain stuffing without the use of the oven, eggs, or bread.

You only need one skillet for this recipe!

makes: 6-8 servings

1 8-ounce package cracked freekeh
   (1 cup dry, or about 2 cups cooked)
1 package all-natural chicken apple sausage
   (4 links)
1 32-ounce carton of vegetable or chicken
   broth (about 4 cups)
2 carrots, diced fine
2 celery stalks, diced fine

1 medium onion, diced fine
1 teaspoon thyme
2 teaspoons sage, ground or rubbed
1 teaspoon rosemary
¾ cup dried tart cherries
½ cup raw chopped cashews (or chestnuts if
   they are in season)
salt and pepper to taste

options: add 2 tablespoons of butter or butter substitute for additional flavor.

Chop the sausage links into slices and add to a large skillet with a little olive oil. Cook over medium heat until they are browned on all sides. Once done, set aside and add broth to the skillet. Raise the heat to high and add the package of freekeh. Bring the freekeh and broth to a boil, add the vegetables, and reduce heat to low. Add seasonings, cover, and let simmer for about 20 minutes, stirring on occasion. After about 20–25 minutes, toss in the sausage, cherries, and nuts. Add salt and pepper to taste. Serve.

timesaver: don't feel like adding all the spices? Look for Rosemary Sage Freekeh by Freekeh Foods—it's preseasoned and works great in the stuffing.

grilled chicken marinated in yogurt, mint, and lemon

You can grill the eggplant and zucchini as well as the chicken and tomatoes if you wish! Or simply roast them in the oven.

I eat this dish at room temperature with fresh tomatoes, but roasted tomatoes would be delicious, too! Top with a little extra yogurt that has been seasoned with garlic, mint, and lemon.

makes: 4-6 servings

1 8-ounce package cracked freekeh
   (1 cup dry, or about 2 cups cooked)
2½ cups chicken broth or vegetable broth
2 chicken breasts, skinless, deboned
½ eggplant, sliced thin in long strips
1 medium zucchini, sliced thin
1 large tomato, diced
½ onion, diced
a few shakes of oregano
a few shakes of red pepper flakes
good-quality extra virgin olive oil

fresh mint
freshly squeezed lemon juice
sea salt and fresh black pepper

marinade for the chicken:
1 cup plain Greek yogurt (I used 0% fat yogurt)
about 4 cloves garlic, minced
1 lemon, juiced
fresh mint

timesaver: look for a bag of frozen grilled
   vegetables in the market!

Cut up chicken into 1-inch, bite-sized pieces. Mix the marinade ingredients together in a bowl. Add the chicken and cover tightly. Place in refrigerator for at least 4 hours or, even better, overnight.

Pour the broth in a saucepan, add the freekeh, and bring to a boil, cooking for 1 minute. Reduce heat to low. Cover and simmer for about 25 minutes.

You can cook the chicken, zucchini, and eggplant either on a traditional outdoor grill or on an indoor electric grill (like a George Foreman Grill®), or cook it in the oven. To grill outside, place the chicken chunks on skewers and cook until done. For the eggplant and zucchini, drizzle a little olive oil, salt, and pepper on a plate and dip the vegetables in it to coat. Add them to the grill and cook on both sides until tender. Set aside. If desired, you can cook tomato wedges or cherry tomatoes and purple onion on the grill, too.

Once the freekeh is done, put it in a large bowl. Remove the chicken from the skewers and add them to the bowl. Cut up the vegetables into bite-sized pieces and add them. Add in oregano, freshly squeezed lemon juice, salt, pepper, and chopped mint. Serve with a dollop of a new batch of yogurt seasoned in the same way as the marinade. Garnish with a few black olives.

Italian sausage with sweet pepper freekeh

Perfect for those impromptu summer gatherings or tailgating parties. Whole Foods has amazing all-natural varieties of sausages with no added nitrates or nitrite preservatives. They have some unusual blends that are worth looking for—like the spinach and feta sausage.

makes: 4-6 servings (or 1 link per person)

1 bag of tricolored frozen peppers, thawed and patted dry

1 8-ounce package cracked freekeh (1 cup dry, or about 2 cups cooked)

2½ cups vegetable broth

1 package Italian sausages or any kind of sausage (about 6 links)

a dash of turmeric powder (about ¼ teaspoon)

a dash of cumin, ground (about ¼ teaspoon)

dash or two of red chili flakes

salt and pepper to taste

In a large skillet, add freekeh and broth and bring to a boil. Reduce to low and simmer for about 15 minutes. Add in the thawed peppers, turmeric powder, cumin, and red chili flakes and cook on low for an additional 10 minutes or until the freekeh is tender and the liquid is absorbed. Add salt and pepper to taste.

Grill the sausages outside or on an indoor electric grill until cooked through. Serve on the side of freekeh, or dice up and mix into the freekeh.

Serve grilled asparagus or other vegetables on the side.

chapter 6

date
night

flavorful dishes to
spice up the evening

risotto-style freekeh with salmon, morel mushrooms, and asparagus

Hot smoked salmon has a completely different texture from lox. I first tried hot smoked salmon in Seattle at Pikes Place Fish Market. It's flaky and so rich! Look for it nationwide in vacuum-sealed packages in your seafood department. Or, better yet, order it online direct from Washington at jacksfishspot.com or seabear.com.

makes: 4 servings

1 8-ounce package cracked freekeh
   (1 cup dry, or about 2 cups cooked)
2 cups vegetable broth (plus a little more for
   the asparagus)
½ cup cooking sherry
2 garlic cloves, chopped
2–3 tablespoons butter, Earth Balance®,
   or extra virgin olive oil
10 morel mushrooms, fresh or dried and
   rehydrated
about ¼ teaspoon of thyme (I used fresh)

about 3 ounces of hot smoked salmon
   (look for this in the seafood department
   in a vacuum-packed container)
about ¼ cup goat cheese
a sprinkle of good-quality Parmesan cheese
   (optional)
6–8 stalks of fresh asparagus, cut into 2-inch
   pieces (only use the top, tender portion of
   the asparagus)
salt and pepper to taste

Pour broth and sherry in a large skillet, add the freekeh, and bring to a boil, cooking for 1 minute. Add garlic and butter or olive oil. Reduce heat to low. Cover and simmer for about 20 minutes. Add in the morel mushrooms and continue to cook for another 5 minutes or until the liquid is absorbed and the freekeh is tender.

While the freekeh is cooking, pour about ½ inch of water or vegetable broth into a large skillet over medium to high heat. Once hot, reduce down to medium and add asparagus. Cover and cook asparagus until tender—about 5–8 minutes.

Once the freekeh is done, toss in the asparagus, cheese, and thyme. Mix carefully and add salt and pepper to taste. Add shreds of the hot smoked salmon and mix through carefully so as not to break up the pieces too much. Serve immediately.

Add a dusting of Parmesan cheese for extra tang if desired.

Thai red curry stir fry with shrimp

makes: 4 servings

1 8-ounce package cracked freekeh
   (1 cup dry, or about 2 cups cooked)
2½ cups vegetable broth
2–3 tablespoons toasted sesame seed oil or
   coconut oil
1 medium onion or 3 spring onions, diced
1–2 sweet peppers, sliced
2–3 carrots, sliced
1½ cups broccoli, chopped

1½ cups fresh sugar snap peas, whole
1 4-ounce jar or can of Thai red curry paste
1 12-ounce can low-fat coconut milk
2–3 limes, juiced
1 tablespoon reduced-sodium soy sauce
1–2 tablespoons fish sauce
4–6 cloves garlic, diced
fresh cilantro, for garnish
chopped peanuts or cashews, for garnish

topping options: chopped peanuts or cashews and cilantro are great to complete this dish.

Pour 2½ cups of broth and the freekeh in a saucepan and bring to a boil, cooking for 1 minute. Reduce heat to low. Cover and simmer for about 25 minutes until the freekeh is tender.

While the freekeh is cooking, in a separate skillet, heat up oil over medium to high heat. Be careful not to burn the oil. Toss in all the vegetables and garlic and stir rapidly. Reduce temperature to medium and cook until the vegetables are slightly tender.

In a separate small saucepan, pour in coconut milk and red curry paste and simmer on medium heat until the ingredients are blended together. In the skillet with the vegetables, add in all the spices and simmer a minute longer. Pour coconut curry mixture in with the vegetables and serve immediately over freekeh as you would a rice dish, or blend the cooked freekeh right into the skillet. Once mixed, serve onto plates and squeeze fresh lime juice on top. Garnish with fresh cilantro and chopped peanuts or cashews.

optional: if you have leftover Kaffir lime leaves from the larb gai recipe on page 162, chop some up and add into this dish for an even more authentic Thai flavor. Or add a little lemongrass paste and a touch of honey to the coconut curry mixture for an even brighter flavor!

flat-iron steak with jerk spices and vegetables

makes: 2-3 servings

about 1 cup of cooked freekeh, made ahead of time (about ½ cup before cooking)
5 ounces flat-iron steak
½ an onion, any kind, chopped
1 medium zucchini, sliced thin lengthwise (or look for frozen grilled marinated zucchini)
½ sweet pepper, chopped
2–3 tablespoons of Caribbean jerk seasoning (note: different brands are spicier than others, so use the amount of spice you know you can handle!)
extra virgin olive oil or garlic-seasoned olive oil
sea salt, black pepper
2–3 teaspoons butter or Earth Balance Butter Spread®
2–3 cloves garlic, chopped

optional: top with a little chopped cilantro or parsley and a squirt of lime.

Make the freekeh ahead of time, or use some that's left over.

Rub the steak with a little olive oil and jerk spices and allow to marinate for about 30 minutes.

Drizzle a little olive oil in a skillet and heat up over medium heat. Add in onion, zucchini, peppers and garlic. Cook for 4–6 minutes or until tender. Season with salt and pepper to taste. Once done, turn heat off and set aside.

In another skillet, melt butter on medium-high heat. Immediately add the whole steak and sear for about 2 minutes on each side for medium. While cooking, tip the pan slightly and collect the butter with a spoon and pour it back onto the steak several times while cooking. After about 2 minutes, turn over and cook about another 2 minutes, and remove from heat. Set on a cutting board and allow to rest a few minutes before cutting into strips.

In a separate container, heat up the precooked freekeh and add in a little olive oil. Once warmed through, mix in with the vegetables and steak and serve.

optional: great served with a little mango salsa on top.

pork cutlets with honey mustard glaze

You will need an oven-proof skillet for this two-step recipe. I really like the Maille Honey Dijon Mustard® in this recipe—it's smooth, spicy sweet and doesn't contain white wine like some Dijon mustards do.

preheat oven: 400°
makes: 4 servings

1 8-ounce package cracked freekeh
   (1 cup dry, or about 2 cups cooked)
2½ cups chicken broth or water
4–6 pork cutlets
2 teaspoons thyme
2 teaspoons honey
3 teaspoons extra virgin olive oil

1 sweet onion, cut into thin wedges
4 garlic cloves, chopped
¼ cup honey mustard (I really like Maille
   Honey Dijon®)
salt and fresh cracked pepper to taste
garnish with fresh chopped parsley or fresh
   thyme

Pour 2½ cups of broth and the freekeh in a saucepan and bring to a boil, cooking for 1 minute. Reduce heat to low. Cover and simmer for about 25 minutes.

While the freekeh is cooking, preheat oven to 400°. Drizzle olive oil on the pork, dust with the thyme, and set aside. In a bowl, mix the honey with mustard and set aside. Over high heat, add a little olive oil to an oven-proof skillet. Add the onion and garlic and cook for about 1 minute. Add pork chops and brown—about 2 minutes on each side. Add the honey mustard mixture to the pan, stirring constantly for another minute or so.

Remove from stovetop and place skillet in oven for about 7 minutes until ingredients are fully cooked. At this point, the sauce will have become a glaze on the pork chops. Once done, remove from heat, place freekeh on plate, and top with the pork chops. Drizzle glaze and onions on top, sprinkle with garnish, and serve immediately.

spicy shrimp soup with gaujillo chili peppers

This was inspired by a recipe from Glenn Castman of Four Seasons Resort, Mexico.

makes: about 4-6 servings

½ cup cracked freekeh
3 cups chicken broth or vegetable broth
1 12-ounce can fire-roasted diced
    tomatoes with green chilis (or look
    for the garlic variety)
6 cloves garlic, sliced
2–3 large red gaujillo chili peppers,
    seeded and diced (or for milder flavor,
    try just 2 first)
1 pound of medium or large shrimp, peeled
    and deveined

½ sweet red pepper
½ yellow pepper
1 medium onion, any kind (I use yellow)
1 teaspoon salt
2–3 teaspoons extra virgin olive oil
fresh cracked pepper
2–3 tablespoons butter or Earth Balance®
    vegan spread
fresh lime wedges
extra water if needed

In a large pot, pour the freekeh and chicken broth and bring to boil over high heat. Once boiling, reduce heat to low. Add in the fire-roasted tomatoes, garlic, diced gaujillo chili peppers, onion, and olive oil. Stir ingredients in and cover. Cook for about 15 minutes, then add in sweet red and yellow peppers and cook further for another 10 minutes or until the freekeh is tender.

In a large skillet, heat up olive oil and saute shrimp for about 3 minutes. Once they begin to turn pink, reduce heat slightly, add the butter, and continue to stir. Shrimp is fully cooked when completely pink. Once done, immediately add them to the soup and serve at once. Serve each bowl with fresh lime wedges. Season to taste.

Garnish with chopped cilantro and a dollop of Mexican crema, nonfat Greek-style yogurt, or low-fat sour cream.

freekeh sushi

Freekeh doesn't contain a lot of gluten or starch, so it's not very sticky. But if you are looking to add more complex carbs into your meal, it's a good replacement for rice in this recipe or others.

makes: about 8–10 freekeh rolls, depending on size

1 8-ounce package cracked freekeh
 (1 cup dry, or about 2 cups cooked)
2½ cups vegetable broth
1 teaspoon ginger powder
6 tablespoons rice vinegar
2 tablespoons rice flour

2 teaspoons arrowroot powder
nori seaweed sushi sheets
sliced carrots, avocado, radish
optional: cooked shrimp, cut into bite-sized
 pieces

Pour freekeh and 2½ cups of vegetable broth into a saucepan and bring to a boil for about a minute. Add the ginger and rice vinegar. Reduce to low heat.

While freekeh is cooking, mix a few teaspoons of water with the rice flour and arrowroot in a small bowl. Add to the freekeh mixture. Cover and simmer for about 25 minutes until the freekeh is tender. Once cooked, remove from heat and place in refrigerator until cool. In the meantime, slice up your vegetables.

Place a sushi mat or a clean cloth napkin on a dry surface and lay a piece of nori on top of it, shiny side down.

Spread freekeh evenly over the nori with your hands, leaving a ½-inch strip of nori uncovered at the bottom.

Place a small amount of filling along the strip on the edge closest to you.

Using the rolling mat, begin to tightly roll the sushi. Start at the side nearest to you and roll away from you.

Be sure to separate the mat from the sushi roll as you go.

When the sushi is completely rolled, add a little warm water with your fingertips to the far inside edge of the nori, and use that to seal the roll firmly together.

Wrap the rolling mat over the top and squeeze to make sure the sushi is rolled nice and tight. With a sharp knife, slice the sushi into six or eight pieces. Serve with dipping sauce.

dipping sauce options: sriracha, wasabi, low-sodium soy sauce, hoisin sauce

scallops with mango puree

Enjoy these scallops with a simple batch of sugar snap peas or snow peas cooked in a little coconut oil or toasted sesame seed oil.

makes: 2 servings

for the freekeh:
½ cup freekeh (makes about 1 cup cooked)
1 cup vegetable broth
2 teaspoons coconut oil (if you have it—if not, skip it)
2 cloves garlic, minced

for the scallops:
8–10 sea scallops (about 4 per person depending on size), patted dry with a paper towel
about 3 tablespoons butter

sea salt and fresh ground black pepper

for the sauce:
1–2 fresh mangoes (the best ones are the little yellow ataulfo mangoes, also known as champagne mangoes when they are in season)
¼ teaspoon lemon or orange zest
about 2 teaspoons freshly squeezed lemon or orange juice
2–3 tablespoons butter, melted

Pour the vegetable broth and the freekeh in a saucepan and bring to a boil, cooking for 1 minute. Reduce heat to low. Add in the coconut oil and garlic. Cover and simmer for about 25 minutes until the freekeh is tender.

Remove the skin and seed from the mango. In a mixer or food processor, blend mango, melted butter, lemon or orange zest, a dash of salt, and the orange or lemon juice until pureed. Transfer to a small saucepan and cook over low heat, stirring often. Then set aside.

Rinse the scallops to remove any grit. Pat dry with a paper towel. Remove the side muscle (some scallops come with this small, tough muscle removed already).

Heat a small skillet over medium-high heat. Add the butter and, once it melts and coats the bottom, immediately add the scallops one at a time with flat side down. Leave them undisturbed for about 2–3 minutes until the bottom edge becomes golden brown. Add salt and pepper, then carefully turn each scallop over and cook an additional 2–3 minutes on that side. Add a little more salt and pepper. The scallops will be done when they become slightly firm to the touch. Once scallops are done, remove skillet from heat and set aside. Add sauce to the plate, and place scallops on top. Place a biscuit cutter on the plate and press freekeh into it. Slowly lift the biscuit cutter off, creating a mound of freekeh. Garnish with diced spring onion or chives, and serve with fresh lemon wedge if desired.

roasted zucchini and portobello mushroom stack with fire-roasted red pepper puree

This may look hard, but it really isn't. I found some beautiful microgreen arugula to sprinkle around the dish that was so pretty! Look for any kind, or simply chop fresh basil or parsley to garnish the plate.

makes: 2 servings (or simply double this recipe now so you can enjoy it the next day, too!)
preheat oven: 350°

½ cup cracked freekeh

1 cup vegetable broth

⅓ cup cooking sherry or other sweet wine, like Marsala

1 medium zucchini, sliced into thin, long strips

1–2 large portobello mushrooms, stems removed

1 small to medium purple onion, sliced into thin pieces

2 tablespoons Parmesan or Asiago cheese

about ½ cup goat cheese

2 teaspoons butter

fresh cracked pepper and just a little sea salt or pink salt

2 fire-roasted red peppers (they come in a jar, usually near pickles and black olives)

a few dashes of Italian seasoning

garnish: microgreens or chopped parsley or basil

Place the zucchini, discs of onion, and mushrooms on a baking sheet. Drizzle a little olive oil on the vegetables. Add salt and fresh cracked pepper and sprinkle Italian seasoning over top. Roast vegetables in oven for about 25 minutes or until tender.

While the vegetables roast, cook the freekeh. Pour broth, sherry, and freekeh in a skillet or saucepan and bring to a boil over high heat. Then cover, reduce heat to low, and simmer for about 20–25 minutes until tender. Once done, set aside.

In a blender or food processor, puree peppers with a little olive oil. Once blended, heat up in a saucepan to warm through.

Once the sauce is done, return the freekeh to the stove in the same skillet. Dice the roasted mushrooms and add to the skillet. Add butter, Parmesan, and about 3 tablespoons of goat cheese. Cook over medium heat for about 2–3 minutes just to melt the cheese, stirring occasionally. Toss in a little chopped parsley or basil if you have some on hand.

Place a biscuit cutter in the center of a plate. Press the freekeh mushroom mixture into it and pack it down with the back of a spoon. Cut the zucchini into about 2-inch long pieces and place them on top of the freekeh until there's about a ½-inch thick stack of zucchini. Carefully remove the biscuit cutter. Dice the roasted onion and place on top of the stack. Sprinkle a few pieces of goat cheese on top of the stack. With a serving spoon, ladle the sauce around the stack, creating a moat. Sprinkle microgreens or diced fresh herbs around the plate. Add fresh cracked pepper on top and serve at once!

note: if you don't have a biscuit cutter, simply mound and shape with your hands, pressing firmly enough to allow for the shape to remain intact while assembling the rest of the dish.

larb gai salad

Larb gai is known as a traditional Thai street food. This tangy, spicy dish is one of my favorites. Kaffir lime leaves are a key flavor in this recipe, and I've found them in Asian markets and lots of regular grocery stores in the produce department with the other herbs.

makes: 4-6 servings

1 8-ounce package cracked freekeh
  (1 cup dry, or about 2 cups cooked)
4½ cups chicken broth
2 large chicken breasts, skinless, deboned
  (or about 3 small breasts)
2 fresh Kaffir lime leaves, chopped
  (look for these in the fresh produce area
  or Asian market)
3–4 small fresh red or green chilis, seeded
  and chopped fine (I used red Thai chilis)
about ½ red onion, chopped fine
2–3 spring onions, chopped fine

3 tablespoons fish sauce
2 teaspoons coconut sugar (or another
  granulated sugar)
4 cloves fresh garlic, minced
3 large limes, juiced
½ bunch cilantro, about 1½ cups, chopped
½ cup fresh mint, chopped
fresh grape tomatoes, sliced in half
about 1 cup shredded carrot
serve with romaine hearts, iceberg lettuce, or
  butter lettuce leaves

Pour 2½ cups of the chicken broth and the freekeh in a saucepan and bring to a boil, cooking for 1 minute. Reduce heat to low. Cover and simmer for about 25 minutes until the freekeh is tender.

In a medium saucepan, add about 2 cups of chicken broth and the chicken breasts. If needed, add water to have enough liquid to cover the breasts. Bring to a boil, then reduce heat to medium and simmer until chicken is fully cooked. If desired, quarter chicken breasts prior to cooking. Once cooked, remove the chicken and allow to cool on a cutting board for a few minutes. Once cooled slightly, mince the chicken with a sharp knife, or use a food processor to grind the chicken into fine pieces. Then set aside and allow to cool to room temperature, or, if you prefer, chill in the refrigerator.

While the chicken is cooking, prepare the dressing. In a small bowl, add the lime juice, chopped chili peppers, kaffir lime leaves, lime juice, garlic, fish sauce, sliced onion, spring onion, and coconut sugar. Mix well with a spoon until the sugar is dissolved.

In a large bowl, toss in the ground chicken, shredded carrot, tomatoes, cilantro, and mint. Pour in the dressing and mix with a spoon to coat all ingredients. Taste and add more lime or fish sauce as desired. Serve with hearts of romaine lettuce leaves and the freekeh on the plate.

To enjoy this dish using your hands, add freekeh to a lettuce leaf and top with the chicken mixture.

pistachio-encrusted shrimp with broccoli slaw

These shrimp have been a favorite among my friends for a long time. I hope you enjoy them too.

makes: 2 servings
preheat oven: 450°

10–12 large fresh shrimp (I have tried frozen and it doesn't work as well)
2 egg whites
about 1 cup pistachios (I used raw, shelled, unsalted)
½ cup cracked freekeh
1 cup vegetable broth or water
2 cloves of garlic, chopped
¼ teaspoon dry ginger
a few shakes of tamari or low-sodium soy sauce

1 small bag of broccoli slaw or about 2 cups shredded cabbage and carrot
2 tablespoons rice vinegar
drizzle of toasted sesame seed oil
black pepper
garnish options: diced sweet red or yellow peppers, sprinkles of chopped cilantro, spring onion, or microgreens
dash red pepper flakes or cayenne pepper (optional)

Pour broth and the freekeh in a saucepan and bring to a boil, cooking for 1 minute. Reduce heat to low. Add garlic and dry ginger. Cover and simmer for about 25 minutes until the freekeh is tender.

Prepare the shrimp by removing the shells. Remove tail if desired. Devein and butterfly the shrimp with a sharp knife. Rinse shrimp and pat dry with a paper towel. In a food processor or blender, grind the pistachios to the consistency of breadcrumbs Be careful not to make the pistachios too fine, or they will be harder to work with. Place shrimp on a plate. Take the egg whites and whisk them with a piece of ice to keep them very cold. Once egg whites are whisked, remove ice cube. With your right hand, dip the shrimp fully into the egg whites. Then place it over top of the plate of ground pistachios. Rather than dipping the shrimp into the plate, use your left hand to sprinkle pistachios over the shrimp, making sure to coat it entirely. Once done, place on a baking sheet lined with parchment paper, if you have it. Continue doing this until all the shrimp are coated. Bake in the oven for 7–10 minutes until shrimp are firm and pink on the edges. While they cook, begin preparing the slaw.

Heat up a little drizzle of sesame oil in a skillet over medium heat. Toss in the broccoli slaw and stir-fry for only about 2 minutes, until the vegetables are wilted yet still crisp. Remove from heat immediately and toss in the rice vinegar. Add a dash of red pepper flakes or cayenne pepper if desired. Set aside.

Place freekeh in the center of the plate. Add a generous portion of broccoli slaw. Top with 4–5 shrimp and garnish with cilantro or other chopped greens. Sprinkle finely chopped red and yellow sweet peppers if you have them. Enjoy immediately.

tip: these shrimp work great on their own as a party hors d'oeuvre. Once dusted with pistachio, place the raw shrimp on a baking sheet and freeze them. Once frozen, you can transfer them to a sealed freezer-proof container for up to a week. Then when you have your party, preheat the oven to 450°, place shrimp on a cookie sheet, and cook for 8–11 minutes until done! To make a nice Asian dipping sauce, add about a teaspoon of granulated sugar (I like coconut palm sugar) to ½ cup of rice vinegar and heat a little in the microwave until the sugar is dissolved. Add a few shakes of red chili flakes or a small diced Thai red chili and place in a pretty bowl in the center of a tray of shrimp.

chapter 7

one-pot
meals

soups and meals that can
be made in one single
skillet or pot, no kidding

chicken sausage soup
with cannellini beans

You can make this on top of the stove in a large skillet or cook it in a crock-pot while you're at work! For the crock-pot version, dice up the sausage first and brown it on top of the stove. Then add it to the crock-pot with all the top ingredients except the beans, and allow it to cook all day while you are at work. Prior to serving, add the beans and garnish, and it's dinnertime!

makes: about 6 servings

Measurements are approximate—as with many soups, you can add more or less depending on what you enjoy.

2 tablespoons olive oil
3–4 chicken sausage links (I used the Whole Foods chicken feta spinach variety!)
2 carrots, chopped
1 14.5-ounce can crushed tomatoes or fire-roasted tomatoes in garlic and olive oil
1 medium onion, any kind, chopped
½ cup freekeh (or about 1 cup cooked)
4 cups chicken broth or vegetable broth
1 teaspoon oregano

2 teaspoons mild chili powder (or 2 diced and seeded guajillo peppers)
salt and pepper to taste
1 15-ounce can white cannellini beans, rinsed and drained

garnish:
crumbled feta cheese
a little fresh or frozen spinach, thawed, with water pressed out

In a large skillet or pot, drizzle the olive oil. Over medium heat, brown the diced sausage, turning to brown on all sides. Once done, remove them, break into pieces, and set aside.

Combine all ingredients except for the beans in the same skillet or pot and simmer over medium heat until it begins to heat through. Simmer for about 30 minutes or so. Add in the beans and continue to cook for another 10 minutes or longer.

Season with salt and pepper to taste. Serve in a bowl and top with a little cooked spinach and a few crumbles of feta or goat cheese. Serve immediately.

Greek chicken

Using fresh herbs makes this dish come alive. If you aren't already growing your own herbs, they are so easy to grow on your patio or in your kitchen window! Look for small starter plants at your plant nursery in spring and you can enjoy the herbs in lots of recipes.

makes: 4-6 servings

2½ cups vegetable broth or chicken broth

1 8-ounce package cracked freekeh
(1 cup dry, or about 2 cups cooked)

1 12.5-ounce can fire-roasted diced tomatoes in garlic and olive oil (or any kind of diced tomatoes)

1 small onion

1 tablespoon fresh oregano or 2 tablespoons dried oregano

4 cloves garlic, diced

1 teaspoon fresh marjoram

1 teaspoon fresh thyme

2 chicken breasts, skinless, boneless, cut into chunks

2 medium zucchini, chopped in large pieces

1–2 small or medium yellow squash, chopped in large pieces

1 4-ounce package of feta cheese

sea salt, fresh cracked pepper to taste

a dash or two of red chili flakes or cayenne pepper

In a large skillet, add the first eight ingredients and heat on high until mixture nearly boils. Then reduce down to medium, add chicken, and cover. Allow to simmer about 20 minutes, stirring occasionally and making sure the chicken is covered with liquid to keep it from drying out.

Add the zucchini, squash, and crumbled feta and cover. Allow to cook for about 10 minutes or more. Once chicken is fully cooked and vegetables are tender, it's done.

lemon dill chicken with carrots

Somewhere along the way, growing up, I decided that I didn't like the color pink, white dresses, or the flavor of dill. I still don't like dresses, but I do love dill! And Pink? Well, I do workouts to her music now. Does that count as a "like"?

makes: 4 servings

1 8-ounce package cracked freekeh
   (1 cup dry, or about 2 cups cooked)
2–3 tablespoons olive oil
1 medium onion, diced
2–3 cups carrots, sliced in 2-inch pieces
4–6 garlic cloves, diced

4 tablespoons butter or extra virgin olive oil
2½ cups chicken broth
3–4 chicken breasts, whole, skinless, boneless
1 bunch fresh dill (about 1 cup), chopped
2 lemons, juiced
fresh cracked pepper and salt to taste

In a large skillet, heat up olive oil over medium heat. Toss in carrots, onions, and garlic and cook for about 5 minutes or until the onions are translucent. Add olive oil or butter to skillet and add in uncooked freekeh. Stir to coat freekeh. Add chicken broth. Place chicken in the liquid with the freekeh and vegetables. Top with the dill and the juice of one lemon. Cover and reduce heat to low. Cook for an additional 20–30 minutes or until the chicken is done. Add a little dill and cracked pepper, plus the rest of the lemon juice, and serve.

optional: for extra bite, add whole green peppercorns during cooking.

red yam stew with kale, pinto beans and fire-roasted tomatoes

I shared a variation of this recipe at my very first Get Bon Retreat in 2011 that I hosted. I shared some great fun teaching folks how to cook my recipes and had fun working out in the woods with the participants.

It's a simple recipe that you can also prepare easily in a crock pot; and make endless variations by adding chicken or other types of beans.

preheat oven: 375°
makes: 6-8 servings

1 8-ounce package cracked freekeh
   (1 cup dry, or about 2 cups cooked)
3 red yams, scrubbed rinsed, cut into 1-inch
   cubes (leave skins on if desired)
4 cups vegetable broth
2 bay leaves
1 bunch of fresh lacinato kale, cut into
   bite-sized pieces (also called flat leaf
   Dinosaur Kale)

1 small onion, diced
2 teaspoons mild chili powder
1 12-ounce can pinto beans, rinsed and
   drained
1 12-ounce can fire-roasted tomatoes, or
   canned diced tomatoes
2–3 garlic cloves, diced

Scrub the yams and cut into 1-inch cubes. Place yams on a foil-lined baking sheet and drizzle a little olive oil on them. Bake in 375° oven for about 25 minutes or until tender. Remove from oven and set aside. While the yams are cooking, pour all remaining ingredients into a large pot on top of the stove over high heat. Stir with a spoon and heat for about 5 minutes. Reduce heat to low and add roasted yams. Cover partially and simmer for at least 30 minutes. Check occasionally and give a stir. Continue to cook longer for richer flavor, adding water or more broth if desired.

In a large pot on the stove, add all all ingredients except for pinto beans and kale. Allow to nearly boil, then reduce down to simmer over low heat and cover for about 20 minutes.

Then, remove lid, and taste test. Add more chili powder or seasoning if desired. Add pinto beans and kale. Cook for another 10 minutes and serve.

options: Sprinkle a little nutritional yeast on top for a "parmesan cheese" flavor without the fat.

Substitute diced skinned pumpkin, butternut squash, or sweet potatoes instead of yams in this recipe.

This can also be prepared in a crock pot.

chicken soup with mushrooms, black japonica rice, and freekeh

Black Japonica rice has a nutty mushroom-like flavor. It's also a gorgeous purplish color! Black Japonica rice has become more and more widely available in the grocery aisle on its own and in various rice blends.

You can prepare this in a crock pot as well. Simply toss all ingredients in and cook away!

makes: 6 servings

1 8-ounce package cracked freekeh
   (1 cup dry, or about 2 cups cooked)
1 cup black japonica rice
1 cup carrots, diced
2 large leeks, diced
1½ teaspoons thyme
1 teaspoon oregano
1 teaspoon sage
½ teaspoon dried mustard

15 garlic cloves, diced (trust me!)
2 bay leaves
2 cups chicken broth (1 16-ounce Tetra® pack*)
4 cups mushroom broth (1 32-ounce
   Tetra® pack)
1 cup cooking sherry
1 cup water
4 whole chicken breasts, skinless, boneless

Place all ingredients except for the water and sherry in a large pot and bring to a boil. Reduce heat, cover, and simmer for 30 minutes. Add in the sherry. Continue to simmer for 30 minutes more. If the chicken breasts haven't naturally broken apart into pieces, break them into bite-sized pieces with a fork. Remove lid slightly, add the water, and cook for about 15 minutes. The longer you cook the soup, the richer the flavor will be.

*Tetra® packs are shelf-stable cartons of broth.

hearty beef stew

Here's another one-pot meal that you can make in the oven or crock-pot. The aroma is guaranteed to drive you and your dog nuts! Add whatever root vegetables you have in your refrigerator. You can do no wrong with this one. Easy peasy.

preheat oven: 300°
makes: 4-6 servings

1 8-ounce package cracked freekeh
   (1 cup dry, or about 2 cups cooked)
1 to 1½ pounds of beef stew meat, cubed
   (I use grass-fed beef)
3–4 tablespoons extra virgin olive oil
32 ounces beef broth
2 cups mushrooms, sliced
1 cup onions, cut into wedges
2 cups carrots cut into discs
   (add more if desired)
1 cup red wine
½ cup tomato paste
4 whole garlic cloves

3 bay leaves
1 teaspoon paprika
½ teaspoon onion powder
½ teaspoon dried mustard
¼ teaspoon cumin
1 teaspoon thyme
1 teaspoon ground rosemary
a shake of red pepper flakes or cayenne
   pepper
4 good cranks of fresh black pepper
salt to taste
1 small bag of frozen peas (about 1½ cups)

In a large, oven-proof pot, heat olive oil over medium heat. Toss in beef and brown on all sides. The beef doesn't have to be cooked all the way through, just browned on the outside to seal in moisture. Once browned, remove beef and set aside. In the same pot on medium heat, add a little more oil and toss in onions, carrots, and mushrooms and cook for 5 minutes until onions are translucent. Remove from heat and add beef back into the pot. Add tomato paste, red wine, spices, uncooked freekeh, and broth, stirring. Cover with lid and cook in the preheated oven. Check in 1 hour and give a little stir. The liquid should be almost fully absorbed by the freekeh. Add in frozen peas. Place lid back on and continue cooking an additional 30 minutes.

optional: parsnips, sun chokes, or rutabagas are great in this recipe, too.

savory herb-baked chicken with root vegetables

You may be surprised to find prunes in the ingredient list, but when cooked, they create a nice sweet sauce that balances nicely with the savory herbs.

preheat oven: 400°
makes: 4 servings

1 8-ounce package cracked freekeh
   (1 cup dry, or about 2 cups cooked)
2½ cups chicken broth
2–3 chicken breasts, skinless, boneless, cut
   into cubes
4–6 carrots, cut in half
2–4 parsnips, cut in half

1 medium onion, cut in wedges
6 garlic cloves, peeled, whole
1 cup prunes, pitted (about 15)
1 tablespoon olive oil
1 package of fresh poultry herb blend (or 2–3
   sprigs of fresh rosemary, thyme and sage)
salt and pepper to taste

Add all ingredients to a large, oven-proof pot. If you're using fresh herbs, just toss them, stem and all, right into the pot. Cover and place in oven for about an hour. After an hour, reduce temperature to 350° and cook until the parsnips are tender. Stir and make sure that the chicken remains covered with freekeh and any remaining liquid. Cook another 20–30 minutes. If you like to have your veggies browned, you can remove the lid for the last 10 minutes of cooking time. Just don't let the ingredients get too dry!

optional: if you wish to use bone-in chicken breasts, add 10-15 minutes more of cooking time.

For a variation, try adding in diced rutabagas or turnips when they are available in fall or winter. Be sure to peel the rutabagas before cooking, as they often are covered in a food-grade wax.

freaky freekeh chili

makes: 6 servings

1 8-ounce package cracked freekeh
    (1 cup dry, or about 2 cups cooked)
2 tablespoons olive oil
1 large onion, diced
8–10 garlic cloves, smashed
2 sweet peppers, sliced in 2-inch strips
1 jalapeno, seeded and diced, or ¼ sliced
    poblano pepper
4 tablespoons chipotle powder
    (or chili powder)
1–2 guajillo peppers, seeded and chopped fine
    (optional)
1 teaspoon cumin
1 14.5-ounce can fire-roasted crushed
    tomatoes

1 14.5-ounce can tomato sauce
1–2 cups water
1 15-ounce can aduki beans, pinto beans, or
    black beans, rinsed and drained
fresh cracked pepper and salt to taste
a few shakes of your favorite hot sauce or chili
    sauce

optional garnishes:
avocado, diced
cilantro
plain non-fat Greek-style yogurt
    (instead of sour cream!)

In a pot, toss in olive oil, onion, sweet peppers, and garlic and sauté on medium heat until onions are translucent. Add in all the remaining ingredients and stir. Keep heat on low and continue to cook with lid partially on for about 25 more minutes or longer, if desired. For more flavor, simmer on low for an hour or longer.

optional: add Field Roast Chipotle Vegetarian Sausage® or Tofurkey Kielbasa Vegetarian Sausage® to this recipe! You can find these at Whole Foods and other health food stores. You can also add browned, lean ground turkey to this dish. If you do, you may want to add another 2 cups of tomato sauce or water to keep it moist.

red lentil soup with freekeh, spinach, and za'atar seasoning

makes: 6 servings

1 8-ounce package cracked freekeh
   (1 cup dry, or about 2 cups cooked)
3 cups water
32 ounces vegetable broth
olive oil
1 onion, diced
2 cups carrots, diced
1 cup dry red lentils (also known as dal)
1 cup crushed tomatoes
1 8-ounce bag of fresh spinach, or about 2
   cups of loose spinach

8 garlic cloves, diced
1 teaspoon onion powder
1 teaspoon cumin
1 teaspoon coriander
1 bay leaf, crumbled
½ teaspoon turmeric powder
¾ teaspoon dried ginger or ½ teaspoon fresh
   ginger, minced
3 tablespoons za'atar seasoning
dash of cayenne pepper
sea salt and pepper to taste

Drizzle a little olive oil in a large pot and heat up on medium. Toss in diced garlic, onion, and carrots, and cook for about 2 minutes. Stir in the seasonings and cook for another 2 minutes. Add in freekeh, lentils, tomatoes, vegetable broth, and water. Stir well. Reduce heat to low and cover. Cook for 30 minutes or more. Add more water if desired. Season to taste. Add in spinach and stir until leaves wilt and reduce in volume. Cook for another 5 minutes. Serve with a tablespoon of za'atar spice sprinkled on top.

optional serving suggestion: here's a tasty side dish. Top some whole wheat pita bread with a little olive oil and za'atar seasoning and bake at 300° until crispy.

chapter **8**

let them
eat cake

baked goods mainly
using freekeh flour

warm cardamom-spiced freekeh

It's been said throughout history that cardamom was prized by Egyptian queens. It's a little pricey, so look for it in bulk bins at health food co-ops or in Indian grocery stores, where it will be much less expensive.

If you have some leftover cardamom and pistachios from this recipe, save them and use in the cardamom pistachio cookies with orange zest on page 200.

makes: 4 servings

1 8-ounce package cracked freekeh
   (1 cup dry, or about 2 cups cooked)
1 13.5-ounce can of light coconut milk
2 tablespoons ground cinnamon
½ teaspoon ground cardamom
½ cup honey

1 cup dates, pitted and chopped
4 tablespoons butter or Earth Balance®
2 teaspoons vanilla extract
½ cup pistachios, chopped
   (preferably unsalted)

Pour the coconut milk into a measuring cup and add water until you have 2½ cups of liquid. Add liquid to saucepan. Add freekeh and bring to a boil, cooking for 1 minute. Mix in all other ingredients except for the nuts, and reduce heat to low. Cover and simmer for about 25 minutes. Remove from heat, top with pistachio nuts, and serve immediately.

optional: try adding dried apricots or chopped almonds. Delicious served with yogurt.

biscotti-style chocolate chip hazelnut cookies

My friend, Katrina, inspired this recipe. She's got a knack for baking the best sugar-free things using xylitol instead of refined white sugar. Xylitol is a natural sweetener typically made from birch bark and is also found in various vegetables. It's technically a sugar alcohol but does not contain sugar and does not produce an insulin response in the body when consumed. Therefore, folks say it's a good alternative for people who watch their sugars but enjoy the taste of sweet!

preheat oven: 325°
makes: 18-20 cookies

1¼ cups hazelnut meal or hazelnut flour
   (I used Bob's Red Mill Hazelnut meal/flour,
   available at Whole Foods and natural food
   stores)
1 cup freekeh flour
¼ cup xylitol, coconut sugar, or other
   granulated sweetener

6 tablespoons butter, softened
1 large egg
¾ cup semi-sweet chocolate chips
3 tablespoons cold water,
¼ teaspoon sea salt

In a large bowl, combine freekeh flour, hazelnut meal, xylitol or whatever granulated sweetener you are using, and salt thoroughly. Add softened butter, egg, and cold water and beat with electric mixer until dough is evenly crumbly. Add in chocolate chips.

Using your hands, divide dough in half and form two logs of dough. Place logs on two large sheets of waxed paper or parchment paper. Flatten the top of logs a bit to allow for an oblong shape when sliced into individual biscotti. Wrap the logs in waxed paper and cool in the freezer for 15–20 minutes or in the refrigerator for 2 hours or more. Slice dough into ¼- or ½-inch thick cookies and place about 1 inch apart on a greased cookie sheet.

Bake for 18–20 minutes, or until edges are slightly browned. Store cookies in tin or foil rather than Tupperware®.

carrot apple muffins

These are very moist. Feel free to add even more spices if you'd like.

preheat oven: 350°
makes: 10–12 regular muffins or 6–8 large muffins

1 cup freekeh flour
1 cup almond flour or almond meal (look for
    this in natural grocery stores in bulk bins
    or baking aisle)
3 eggs
¾ cup coconut oil (heated to melt into
    a liquid form)
¾ cup coconut palm sugar or other granulated
    sugar
2 teaspoons vanilla extract
2 teaspoons ground cinnamon

½ teaspoon ground ginger
¼ teaspoon salt
2 teaspoons baking soda
2½ cups carrots, grated (I used about 5–6
    medium-sized carrots)
1 Granny Smith apple, peeled and grated
1 cup ground pecans
1 cup raisins
1 cup almond milk
⅓ cup orange juice

In a large bowl, combine freekeh flour, almond meal, coconut palm sugar, salt, ground ginger, cinnamon, and baking soda. Add eggs, carrots, ground pecans, apple, coconut oil, and raisins, and mix with a spoon.

Add orange juice, vanilla extract, and almond milk until all ingredients are moist. Spoon batter into lined muffin tins, filling to the top. Bake for about 25–30 minutes or until inserted toothpick comes out clean.

optional goat cheese frosting:
1 6-ounce package of goat cheese
¼ cup butter, softened

¼ cup coconut oil (to liquefy hard coconut oil,
    warm in a saucepan on the stove)
¼ cup agave (more or less to suit your taste)
1 teaspoon vanilla extract

In a large bowl, combine all ingredients with an electric mixer. To thicken frosting, place in refrigerator before topping the muffins. Store frosted muffins in a sealed container in refrigerator.

banana freekeh oatmeal bread

This bread has a great texture and flavor. It would also be good topped with a frosting made with cream cheese or the goat cheese frosting recipe on page 192.

preheat oven: 350°

1 cup freekeh flour
1 cup oatmeal (old-fashioned or quick oats)
2 teaspoons baking powder
¼ teaspoon salt
4 large ripe bananas (mashed)
3 large eggs, slightly beaten
½ cup butter, melted

½ cup coconut palm sugar
 (or other granulated sugar)
½ cup honey
1½ tablespoons almond milk, unsweetened,
 or milk
1 teaspoon lemon juice

In a large bowl, combine flour, oatmeal, baking powder, and salt.

Add mashed bananas, melted butter, coconut sugar, honey, eggs, almond milk, and lemon juice. Mix ingredients with a spoon or hand mixer and pour into a greased 5x9-inch loaf pan.

In a preheated oven, bake for 45–50 minutes. Top with foil and bake for another 15 minutes. Bread is done when an inserted knife comes out fairly dry. Note: Because this bread is very moist, the knife will not come out completely clean.

biscotti-style chocolate cookies

makes: about 28 cookies
preheat oven: 325°

1¼ cups hazelnut flour (I used Bob's Red
    Mill Hazelnut Flour®)
1 cup freekeh flour
1 cup xylitol, coconut sugar, or any
    granulated sugar

½ cup butter, softened (one stick)
¼ cup plus 1 tablespoon cold water
⅔ cup unsweetened cacao or cocoa powder
1 cup slivered almonds (optional)
½ teaspoon sea salt

In a large bowl, combine freekeh flour, hazelnut flour, cocoa, xylitol, and salt thoroughly.
Add softened butter and cold water and beat with electric mixer until dough is evenly crumbly.
Add almonds.

Using your hands, divide dough in half and form two logs of dough. Place logs on two large
sheets of waxed paper or parchment paper. Flatten the top of the logs a bit to allow for an oblong
shape when sliced into individual biscotti. Wrap the logs in waxed paper and cool in the freezer
for 15–20 minutes or in the refrigerator for 2 hours or more. Slice dough into ¼- to ½-inch thick
cookies and place about 1 inch apart on a greased cookie sheet.

Bake for 18–20 minutes, or until edges are slightly browned. Store cookies in tin or foil rather
than Tupperware®.

blueberry crumble

My cousins back in Sedley, Virginia, grow the best blueberries! I helped pick them, and I think I ate more of them than I collected! For this recipe, fresh blueberries work best instead of frozen.

preheat oven: 375°
makes: 6-8 servings

filling:
1 teaspoon unsalted butter, softened
2 pints fresh blueberries (you can also use
   frozen, thawed)
¼ cup pure maple syrup (Grade B is best)
1 tablespoon cornstarch
½ cup orange juice
1 teaspoon vanilla extract

topping:
1 cup freekeh flour
½ cup coconut sugar or other
   granulated sugar
¼ cup maple syrup
6 tablespoons butter, cold and cut into cubes
½ cup oats, uncooked
½ cup chopped pecans

In a bowl, add the blueberries, maple syrup, orange juice, and vanilla. In a separate bowl, add a teaspoon of water to cornstarch and mix. Add into the blueberry mixture.

In a large bowl, add the flour, coconut sugar, maple syrup, and butter. Mix well by hand or use an electric mixer. Once it's really crumbly, stir in oats and nuts.

Pour the filling into a 9x12-inch greased baking dish and spread out evenly. Add the topping. Bake uncovered for about 30 minutes or until the topping is golden brown and the edges of the fruit are bubbling. Serve warm or at room temperature.

optional: great served with vanilla Greek yogurt as a healthy creamy topping!

cardamom pistachio cookies
with orange zest

A great little cookie with coffee in the afternoon. These three exotic flavors are so good, it's hard to just eat one cookie at a time!

makes: about 8 cookies, 3 inches wide
preheat oven: 350°

1 cup freekeh flour
1 cup almond meal or almond flour
1 cup butter or Earth Balance®
1 egg yolk
1 tablespoon vanilla
1 teaspoon plus a pinch cardamom, ground
   (I used preground green cardamom, but
   you can get a more fragrant flavor by
   grinding your own from a whole white or
   green cardamom pod)
1 cup pistachios, ground (keep a little out to
   sprinkle on the tops of cookies)
¾ cup coconut palm sugar or other granulated
   sugar
¼ cup coconut oil
½ teaspoon or more of orange zest
dash of salt

Beat the butter and sugar together with a mixer or with a spoon. Add in egg yolk and vanilla extract and beat for another minute.

Slowly add in a little of the almond flour, freekeh flour, ground pistachios, and salt. Continue to mix and beat on a low setting for another minute. Add spices, coconut oil, and orange zest. Continue mixing until the batter is all combined.

Spoon out dough onto a baking sheet lined with parchment paper (optional). Flatten the dough with your fingers slightly, sprinkle more ground pistachios on top, and lightly press the nuts into the dough.

Bake for about 10–12 minutes or until the edges of the cookies begin to get golden brown. Once done, remove from oven and allow to cool before storing in an airtight container.

Note: The cookies will become harder as they cool.

oatmeal raisin cookies
with chia seeds

My dad was an amazing baker. His gooey oatmeal raisin cookies were so good. Now that I'm eating healthier as an adult, this recipe is a healthier version of an old favorite. Chia seeds are incredibly high in omega-3 fatty acids and also add extra fiber and protein to these cookies. Coconut oil adds flavor and is also good for you. Health professionals say coconut oil aids in helping the body burn fat.

makes: about 10 3-inch cookies
preheat oven: 350°

½ cup freekeh flour
½ cup almond meal or almond flour
2 eggs
⅓ cup coconut palm sugar or any granulated
    sugar, such as Turbinado natural sugar
    (which is less processed)
1 cup softened butter (two sticks) or 1 cup
    Earth Balance® spread

1 tablespoon vanilla extract
1 teaspoon baking powder
¾ teaspoon cinnamon, ground
2 tablespoons chia seeds
1½ cups raisins
1½ cups oats (uncooked)
2 tablespoons coconut oil (or vegetable oil)
a dash of salt

In a medium-sized bowl, mix together butter and sugar using an electric mixer or a large spoon.

Add in the eggs, vanilla, baking powder, and cinnamon and mix for about another minute until ingredients are combined.

Slowly add a little of both flours, raisins, dash of salt, and coconut oil until ingredients are combined. Add in chia seeds.

Using a small spoon, drop mounds of the dough onto a baking sheet lined with parchment paper. Flatten the mounds slightly.

Bake on the middle rack of the oven for about 8–10 minutes or until the edges become golden brown.

optional: go nuts! Add in about ½ cup of pecans or walnuts.

Index